SCHOOL CULTURE
RECHARGED

Another ASCD book by
Steve Gruenert and Todd Whitaker:

School Culture Rewired: How to Define, Assess, and Transform It

SCHOOL CULTURE
RECHARGED

STRATEGIES TO ENERGIZE YOUR STAFF AND CULTURE

STEVE GRUENERT
& TODD WHITAKER

 Alexandria, Virginia USA

1703 N. Beauregard St. • Alexandria, VA 22311–1714 USA
Phone: 800-933-2723 or 703-578-9600 • Fax: 703-575-5400
Website: www.ascd.org • E-mail: member@ascd.org
Author guidelines: www.ascd.org/write

Deborah S. Delisle, *Executive Director;* Robert D. Clouse, *Managing Director, Digital Content & Publications;* Stefani Roth, *Publisher;* Genny Ostertag, *Director, Content Acquisitions;* Susan Hills; *Acquisitions Editor;* Julie Houtz, *Director, Book Editing & Production;* Darcie Russell, *Editor;* Georgia Park, *Senior Graphic Designer;* Mike Kalyan, *Director, Production Services;* Keith Demmons, *Production Designer;* Kyle Steichen, *Senior Production Specialist*

All web links in this book are correct as of the publication date below but may have become inactive or otherwise modified since that time. If you notice a deactivated or changed link, please e-mail books@ascd.org with the words "Link Update" in the subject line. In your message, please specify the web link, the book title, and the page number on which the link appears.

PAPERBACK ISBN: 978-1-4166-2345-8   ASCD product #117016
PDF E-BOOK ISBN: 978-1-4166-2347-2; see Books in Print for other formats. Quantity discounts are available: e-mail programteam@ascd.org or call 800-933-2723, ext. 5773, or 703-575-5773. For desk copies, go to www.ascd.org/deskcopy.

ASCD Member Book No. FY17-5. ASCD Member Books mail to Premium (P), Select (S), and Institutional Plus (I+) members on this schedule: Jan, PSI+; Feb, P; Apr, PSI+; May, P; Jul, PSI+; Aug, P; Sep, PSI+; Nov, PSI+; Dec, P. For current details on membership, see www.ascd.org/membership.

Library of Congress Cataloging-in-Publication Data

Names: Gruenert, Steve. | Whitaker, Todd, 1959-
Title: School culture recharged : strategies to energize your staff and
   culture / Steve Gruenert and Todd Whitaker.
Description: Alexandria, Virginia : ASCD, 2017. | Includes bibliographical
   references and index.
Identifiers: LCCN 2016044933 (print) | LCCN 2016045733 (ebook) | ISBN
   9781416623458 (pbk.) | ISBN 9781416623472 (PDF)
Subjects: LCSH: Educational leadership. | School management and organization.
   | School environment. | Educational change.
Classification: LCC LB2805 .G776 2017 (print) | LCC LB2805 (ebook) | DDC
   371.2--dc23
LC record available at https://lccn.loc.gov/2016044933

26 25 24 23 22 21 20 19 18 17   1 2 3 4 5 6 7 8 9 10 11 12

To my wife Emily and our three children,
Jennifer, Mackenzi, and Madison.
Thanks for putting up with my occasional lack of maturity.

—Steve

To my wife Beth and our three children,
Katherine, Madeline, and Harrison.

—Todd

SCHOOL CULTURE RECHARGED

We want you to harness the power of culture and the power of people so that you can develop teachers and schools that are better than ever before.

INTRODUCTION

I n our first book, *School Culture Rewired: How to Define, Assess, and Transform It* (Gruenert & Whitaker, 2015), we tried to make school culture relevant as well as accessible. In other words, we tried to help readers understand what it is, how it might influence teacher behaviors, and how leaders might begin to shape a new culture if the one they have is not working well.

The response to *School Culture Rewired* has been incredible. The degree to which educators understand and care about the culture of their schools and organizations has been awe-inspiring. We have had the pleasure to connect with many readers in person, at presentations around the world, and on social media (Twitter @SteveGruenert and @ToddWhitaker); and, as you will find out in this book, some of you have turned school culture change into a viral phenomenon (#CelebrateMonday).

In this book we try to present a more practical application of how school leaders might use (rather than attack) their cultures to improve their schools and people. We do not want you to just understand the concept; we want you to harness the power of culture and the power of people so that you can develop teachers and schools that are better than ever before.

This book is written as a stand-alone read. It's a little like watching the movie *Fast and Furious 7*. You may appreciate it more if you have seen the previous six movies, but if you missed *Fast and Furious 4*, we bet you can still catch on.

If you have read *School Culture Rewired*, you probably already have thought of ways to improve your organization and the valuable people it comprises. However, we'd like to touch upon a few key points so that everyone is up to speed as we learn how to start recharging and energizing both culture and staff.

In *School Culture Rewired* we presented a model that shows the steps we suggest for leaders as they consider shaping a new school culture (see a slightly modified version in Figure I.1). Once leaders are able to grasp a basic understanding of the concept of school culture, they enter an action research process. A cyclical journey takes them from assessing "who we are" to thinking about "where we want to go," revisiting each step so that the previous experience gives more meaning to the next experience—a concept articulated by John Dewey decades ago (Dewey, 1938).

In Figure I.2 we stay with the basic model and the action research approach, but we have added two ideas: (1) people help shape cultures, and (2) cultures help shape people. You need people to have a culture. One person does not make nor does one person have a culture. And if we spend enough time together, a culture will evolve, like it or not. We believe that if school leaders acknowledge these two points, then this book will make a lot of sense.

FIG I.1 **Shaping a New School Culture**

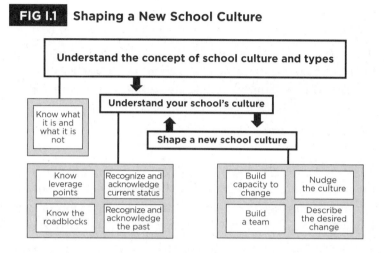

Source: Adapted from *School Culture Rewired: How to Define, Assess, and Transform It* (p. 3), by S. Gruenert and T. Whitaker, Alexandria, VA: ASCD. Copyright © 2015 ASCD. Adapted with permission.

FIG I.2 **Shaping a New School Culture Using People**

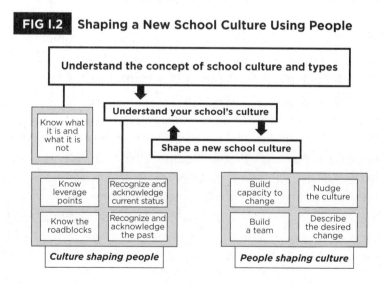

Source: Adapted from *School Culture Rewired: How to Define, Assess, and Transform It* (p. 3), by S. Gruenert and T. Whitaker, Alexandria, VA: ASCD. Copyright © 2015 ASCD. Adapted with permission.

As usual, writing about school culture is a work in progress. It is possible that in the future we may change our minds about some aspects of what we write about. For now, this book represents our best thinking. Writing about culture is not an exact science, and we offer no guarantees, but as we continue to interact with school leaders and review research, this is what makes sense to us.

We have divided this book into three main concepts: (1) using culture to improve schools, (2) using people—your staff—to improve culture, and (3) using culture to improve job satisfaction and morale. We include the notion of using math to see if an algorithm for school culture exists, and we describe how we might make teaching "cool" again. We hope it will all make sense as you try to harness the strongest force out there when it comes to people's behaviors.

Throughout the book we suggest activities and instruments to use as you begin to implement the ideas. Although it comes with no guarantees that you will become a school culture expert, this book will help you gauge whether you are moving in the right direction or not. Consider this simple analogy: We can sit in a plane or a car and not know much about the mechanical processes that make movement possible, but we will know when it moves, slows down, or speeds up.

Enjoy the ride, and please share your thoughts regarding how you use culture to improve people and use people to improve culture. Good reading!

CHAPTER 1

Exploring the
People–Culture
Dynamic

Although most leaders may see culture as a challenge to overcome, we would like to see them use culture as a force to improve schools.

School culture can be an extremely difficult concept to grasp, especially if we are trying to determine or describe the culture of a setting that we have been a part of for a long time. However, even if we can describe the culture, an even bigger challenge is moving it in a positive direction. Inherently, the culture does not want to be altered, and it senses when we try to change any part of it. That resistance makes it difficult to change a culture. We also know that getting people to change is often equally frustrating. People get into comfort zones and may not want to be poked and prodded even if the change will eventually benefit them.

In this book we bring these two challenges together—improving culture and improving people. The two are interconnected. Although most leaders may see culture as a challenge to overcome, we would like to see them use culture as a force to improve schools. And to a large degree, we may have to work on both—people and culture—simultaneously. Let's take a look at the concept of interactions using organizational climate, which may be easier to grasp.

Climate Versus Culture

First, let's agree that climate and culture are not the same thing. Climate is best understood as the attitude of the school building. It is a collective feeling that members are supposed to display in certain situations. It is the difference between Mondays and Fridays; it is the thing that changes when we announce that tomorrow is a snow day. Culture is much bigger than climate. Culture is the personality of the building. It is the professional religion of the group. Culture gives permission to climate to act as it does.

Schools have "subclimates"—for example, a student climate and a teacher climate (there may also be a parent climate, a community climate, and so on). Looking at climates in terms of positive and negative, let's say each one falls somewhere on a scale of 1 to 10, with 10 being the most positive. If your school has a student climate and a teacher climate, they may be different, yet they also are connected. For example, if you have a positive teacher climate (an 8 on the scale) and a negative student climate (a 2 on the scale), it is because the culture of the school accepts that as the norm. If the teachers come to work happy and the students they interact with each day have a negative tone and attitude, some teachers may find this makes their job easier. Remember, the climate is an indicator of the culture; if students are grumpy all the time, it is because that is how the culture has evolved. If teachers are happy in some schools, it may be because the students are not. Climate and culture are not the same thing, but they are connected.

A simplistic example would be if a school decided to allow its students to have soda and candy in their classes. This decision would likely lead to a short-term "happy" bump in the student climate. Students might be more positive and more excited going into classes the next day. However, as you can imagine, teacher climate might deteriorate as a result. Teachers and custodians might have to deal with spills, messes, and distractions, which could negatively affect how they feel about being at school. And at some point, the teachers' frustrations might lead to their treating students in a way that lowers student attitudes (student climate) to a point where the culture has dictated it is supposed to be. We have to be sensitive to the fact that teacher climate and student climate will tend to move toward a pre-established norm or mean. This is the comfort zone, even if some don't like it.

Regardless of structural changes, all subclimates will find a way to return to the norm. If teachers have a lower climate (negative morale) because they believe policies regarding student behavior and discipline do not support them, this belief will obviously dampen their enthusiasm toward teaching and perhaps even affect how safe they feel in their classrooms or school. Many students (though not all) might enjoy this "no limits" approach, and their morale and climate could be high. But as the situation chips away at teacher climate, the teachers' actions toward students will eventually tamp down student climate. As the school puts more and tighter restrictions on student behavior, the teachers may feel more positive, but if the clamps become too restrictive, the student climate will suffer. With student dispositions and attitudes worsening each day, teacher enthusiasm will eventually decline.

A Delicate Balance

The culture–people dynamic is a delicate balance, but if you can discover the right levers and pulleys, you can use one to assist the growth of the other and carefully improve them both so they are synergistic in helping an organization become more successful and collaborative.

The relationship between teacher climate and student climate as described in the examples is comparable to the relationship between culture and people in an organization. The relationship can be negative, in the sense that each can bring the other down in some circumstances. The purpose of this book, however, is to help you understand how culture and people can also raise each other up. In your school, the two components are already influencing each other, and although it will not be easy to take control and lead the culture–people relationship, in some ways you, as a school leader, are already in control. It is essential to know how much the culture of the school is listening to its leader.

/ / / / / / /

In a later chapter we discuss the concept of "leadership by the numbers," which may help as we think about how to strategically and quantifiably improve the culture. If we think of the culture as the sum of the people and the people as the makeup of the culture, it helps us realize the inherent interrelationship between the two. Adding new, talented staff members and continuing to support and grow existing teachers enables the culture to become more productive. As the culture evolves in a positive direction, it helps to improve the quality of its current talent and inherently attracts more capable people to join the effort. Everyone wants to be associated with a winner, and building a positive culture naturally draws more talented and energetic people to the opportunity. Everyone wants to make a difference. Let's start by understanding how culture can be used to improve schools.

CHAPTER 2

Hacking
Culture to
Recharge
Schools

The culture should be the sentry at the door rather than the monster under the bed.

The word *culture*, as in "organizational culture," has become a buzzword. Whether we are discussing politics, religion, or sports, it seems there is a "culture" working behind the scenes, manipulating outcomes. Given this exposure, culture is becoming less "behind the scenes" and more "in your face." During the 20th century, various authors argued that organizations had cultures. During the first part of the 21st century, they talked about how cultures affect performance. Here we take the next step, helping to develop an understanding of how culture can be used to improve an organization and the people in it.

Culture is not something we are stuck with. Culture is something that evolves every day, sometimes at a snail's pace, sometimes in big leaps. We can all agree that it exists and that it wields great power and influence over what people think and do. Nowhere is this more obvious than in schools.

Consider this analogy. Many of us find comfort in knowing that each morning our car will start, that there will be a parking space at the school, that the temperature inside the school will be pleasant, and that the lights will come on. We believe that being able to get through most of our day without many surprises provides us with a better quality of life. Sometimes the whole day can simply run in default mode. We can do exactly the same things over and over without ever questioning whether a better way exists. If everyone does their part, then the culture will provide security. Day after day, the same thing occurs. This is what culture is supposed to do—it is kind of a manager.

Culture is a powerful force because the rules are not written down. The rules are imprinted into our souls as we pledge allegiance to the group, in this case, our schools. It's not a cult, but our school is a professional religion and we believe *it can be used to improve schools.* In other words, we are not just agreeing with previous authors that you need to be aware of your school's culture before making changes, we are suggesting that you let the culture be the catalyst in those changes.

Your School Five Years Ago— and Five Years from Now

When we speak of a school's vision, most people imagine five years into the future. That would mean you are currently living the vision that was developed five years ago. If we were to walk around your school taking photographs, interviewing people, maybe even looking at some student data, and were to show these artifacts to the people in the past, would they feel good about the future? Would you? What mental pictures (this is where the term *vision* comes from) do you have of your school five years from now? If we were able to provide artifacts from the future, what would you hope they would look like?

If a vision is something that exists in people's minds, then that vision will be vulnerable to the culture, because culture is also found in our minds. The future will always be influenced by the past, as expressed in the culture; we can't start at zero each day. The culture is a voting member of every steering committee—we can hear its voice daily.

Although it may seem that we are painting a hopeless picture, as if the culture will always overpower change, our task is to help you see culture as an ally. We want it to have a place at the table, especially once you get the culture you want. We want it to be strong and resistant to personalities, but not to improvement. The culture should be the sentry at the door rather than the monster under the bed. Changing a culture is not going to be easy, and it will be messy (Fullan, 2014). It will start with strong leadership, but the movement cannot happen without a supporting cast.

So go ahead—think about your school five years from now. What do you hope will be different? What stories do you need to start telling today to make it happen?

What Is School Culture?

In *School Culture Rewired* (Gruenert & Whitaker, 2015) we discussed the concept of school culture and how it affects what educators do in schools. We included some instruments to use as leaders try to get a handle on the types of cultures they have in their schools. We also suggested how they might begin to nudge a school's culture closer to the type of culture they wanted.

In our view, the optimal setting for schools to aspire toward is the collaborative school culture. Although this culture will have some common ingredients across schools, it will look different in every location. The collaborative school culture does not come naturally, largely because many teachers tend to be reluctant to ask their peers for help. Traditionally, a trait of strong teachers has been their independence and autonomy as they exercise professional discretion. The collaborative culture does not encourage autonomy. Instead, its essence is an interdependence among professionals.

In Chapter 1 of this book we discussed the relationship between school culture and school climate, pointing out that they are two different things. Because many people believe these two concepts are the same, it is worth taking another stab at clarifying exactly what culture is. See if this explanation helps:

> Anytime a group of people spend a significant period of time together, they will develop roles and expectations for each other. Over time these roles will define each person and give balance to the group as its members attempt to survive the environment. The group will create rules to define who is a member and who is not. Rewards and sanctions will support these rules, usually in the form of peer pressure. There is comfort and predictability as routines and rituals bond the group. Change is not welcome. A culture has been formed.

Let's take pieces from this explanation to make the concept of culture more understandable and practical.

- The phrase "a significant period of time" can be debated because some cultures may develop more quickly than others. It probably takes longer to change a culture than for a new one to develop. Again, some are stronger than others and may be more resistant to change. However, we are pretty sure it will take the best part of a year or two to reach critical mass.

- "Give balance to the group" suggests an organic equilibrium is necessary. Surviving the environment may require stability from people with certain jobs, such as leaders, information gatherers, security enforcers, entertainers, recruiters, and so on. If someone leaves, the departure may cause an imbalance until that role is filled.

- The statement "Change is not welcome" is where culture gets a bad reputation. Without that statement, the explanation had the potential to qualify as a description of an effective organization. The notion of resisting change— good change or bad change—is the reason we have been drawn to understanding culture as school leaders.

What could all this mean for you as a school leader? Given enough time, a group of people will have or will become a culture. A set of unwritten rules determines what it means to be professional in that setting and will prevail over any written policy. Some aspects of school culture will seem weird, including the notion that it is easier to start a new culture than to change a current one, the idea that a few weak long-time teachers need to stay, that even good ideas will not be embraced if they sound like indictments of current practices rather than gentle suggestions for improvement.

Please understand that attempting to change a school culture means messing with the professional religion of other people. It does not consist of simply making a few adjustments. The desired outcome will be one that changes the way decisions are made, problems are solved, and, ultimately, how people feel about working at your school. We hope you will be able give your staff permission to experience joy when they are working with students or each other, whether it is Monday or Friday. We hope the value of collaboration will skyrocket as teachers learn that the best resource for professional development may be the teacher down the hall and that school improvement might happen in less than two minutes, between classes.

The bottom line will be the measure of trust that occurs among the adults in the building. Admitting that you don't know something is sometimes as difficult as admitting you may be the expert. Becoming vulnerable to your peers' expertise can be uncomfortable (Brown, 2015). But that discomfort is just the voice of the culture whispering in your ear. Let's change that narrative to one that supports asking for help.

The Past, Present, and Future as Variables

To help you think about a balanced approach to developing your school's vision, consider dividing a rectangle into three parts: past, present, and future. If you were to envision how you "do" leadership, how would you say that you apportion your time? One-third to each? Two-thirds to the past? Draw a rectangle and divide it into three parts to show how you would ideally apportion your school's time and efforts among the three variables.

To use another analogy, how much time do you spend looking in the rearview mirror as you drive? When driving, you have a large windshield in front of you, as well as a few smaller mirrors strategically located to catch a glimpse of where you have been—or what is approaching from behind. Is it possible to spend too much time looking at the past, worrying about what has happened or what may be overtaking you? Shouldn't you spend the most time and attention on where you are and where you are going? If we return to your rectangle, imagine the space labeled "past" as the time spent looking in the mirror, the spaces labeled as "present" as the time spent looking at the dashboard instruments, and the spaces labeled as "future" as the time spent looking through the windshield. Which space best represents how you drive?

Imagine that rectangle represents your school. The past is the past, the present is current data, and the future is your school's vision. Think about what your school leaders spend time on.

Which part of that rectangle best represents how your school operates, and which represents an optimal approach? Feel free to draw your own rectangle and share this activity with your leadership team and ask them where your school's time should be spent.

We know that the past will always influence the present and the future. The culture of your school will place a strong value on what has been done in the past, which means it will advocate for the adoption of past behaviors (including problems) as the future nears. This inclination is what anthropologists call being "culture bound," or ethnocentric. The idea is that if it worked in the past, then we might be right in using it again. It is common sense. It is logical. It is how we survive. By the way, the culture is strongest when the group is just trying to survive—in defense mode.

Yet the present is not here very long. See? It's gone! What you just read is now in the past, and it is looking for a place in your brain to attach itself. The culture is trying to help you with that placement. If what you read fits into your current belief system, then it is more likely to be saved, and saved as defense for future arguments against change. If it does not fit, then the culture will try to discredit what you read—and your brain may not let those dendrites become very strong. The game is set up to prevent learning, but we can change that.

The future is the big variable that can scare a culture. The future carries a bit of uncertainty that cultures cannot deal with. Thus what happens next needs to look like something that has already happened in the past, so that all behaviors can be catalogued quickly and easily—for example, life is a bunch of nails that need to be hit, so all you need is a hammer. This makes life predictable—no thinking required.

But here is another possibility. If the past is such a strong influence in what we do now and later, perhaps we can use the past to help us improve rather than feel stuck. The past is recorded in many different forms, including documents, videos, and memories. How can we use these assets to build a better culture? How can something that has already happened become a variable? Let's make the past a "player."

Treasurer (2014) shares how failures can be tickets to the next success. It is all in how the leader interprets it. Consider the following popular expressions: Failure is not an option; If we are not failing, we are not trying hard enough. Which one is your school advocating?

Much has been written about how our memories are not perfect recordings of what we have experienced. And some claim that we may adjust what we remember each time we think about it so that the memory fits into our mental models better. In other words, we will change what happened in the past (in our minds) so that we can continue to be who we are. If that is possible, then maybe we can do so for reasons of improvement rather than self-preservation.

Try the following activity to reveal the self-preservation mindset. As an example, we present a few fictional mandates that may change how teachers and staff behave at schools. Most are absurd and are meant to simply loosen the tension that may be inherent in most meetings. The point is to get people laughing at a few silly items and then ask them to develop their own crazy rules that could make "doing education" more fun. Who knows? One might work. Here are our offerings:

- Each teacher is given $1,000 per week to disseminate among peers for any reason.

- Teachers will be given special license plates that allow them to break traffic laws—but only on school days.

- Teachers may wear clothing that is most conducive to learning—in their opinion.

- Teachers may request that the parent or guardian serve the punishment when the child misbehaves.

- State testing is optional; only teachers may request it.

- Teachers will have three writers from Disney to help develop lesson plans.

- All students must perform one hour of custodial duties each week.

- Teachers may select classroom furniture from IKEA.

- Teachers may celebrate successes with wine at faculty meetings.

- School board members shall perform bus duty and lunch duty and attend a professional learning committee (PLC) meeting one day per month.

Now it is your turn. Ask your teachers to brainstorm their craziest mandates. Listen for patterns and for possible solutions to persisting issues. And, listen for the culture to tell you which ones will never work in your school.

///////

Using school culture to improve schools may be a unique approach. School leaders are warned about how controlling school culture can be. Few consider it an ally. We hope this chapter has helped to reveal how school culture can be a big player in school improvement.

CHAPTER 3

Building an
Intentional
Culture

The principal needs to give effective staff permission to leave (virtually) and begin to build the future away from the distractions of ineffective voices.

Knowing that you can use culture to help improve the people within an organization, you need to make sure the quality of the culture is what you *want* it to be. You need to make sure that the culture is a positive and appropriate one to provide guidance for the individuals within it.

As you think about improving schools, using the concept of organizational culture as the lens provides (1) a different way to approach what needs to be done, (2) a clear path regarding when improvement needs to be done and with whom, and (3) information that needs to be in place before you make the first move. This chapter will provide some insights into addressing these challenges. Later in this chapter we will provide an activity that may help you contrast the culture you have with the one you want and determine where the first moves are.

Imagine a school culture as having a given size and shape—one large rectangle (perhaps envision a building) with large blocks at the bottom supporting medium and small size blocks as the building gets taller. Whenever a few teachers leave that building's culture, the overall building stays the same size but has empty spaces, spaces that could have a vacuum effect. Imagine that the teachers who leave that culture begin to build another, smaller culture.

These teachers may have left because the larger culture was not supporting them; they could be effective teachers running from a bad school culture, or ineffective teachers running from a good school culture. Their move to a new culture (imagined as a smaller building) makes their lives a bit less secure because there is safety in numbers and comfort in status quo. If these are effective teachers, the principal will support them as they create a new culture. If these are ineffective teachers, the principal will need to be sure they are too uncomfortable to return.

Now imagine that this movement of teachers did not simply happen but was orchestrated by the principal. That possibility is what this chapter is about.

Before any of this can happen, the principal needs to know who the effective teachers are, create a crack in the culture (a culture buster) that enables them to sneak out, and then create a safe place for them to grow. And once this alternative gets established, it can become a settlement for new teachers to join as they get added to the staff.

Islands of Effective Teachers

In ineffective schools, effective people are already looking for their own island. They may actually be operating on an island by themselves—they just have to have their classroom door closed so no one can tell. They have learned that it is lonely to be by yourself, but if you share your thoughts with others, the culture may try to prevent you from having peace. A culture and the people in it are often threatened by a member of the group who goes outside the existing cultural norms (e.g., a teacher who wants to empower students). This is why effective teachers or people in struggling environments have learned to keep their efforts to themselves.

The principal needs to give effective staff permission to leave (virtually) and begin to build the future away from the distractions of ineffective voices. These effective teachers are not always the "nice" people, or the ones who seem congenial, bring food, set up social events, or dress in a professional manner. Effectiveness goes deeper than that. And if you can't find such people, you will have to hire them.

Cracking the Culture and Building a Safe Place

There are times when the culture is vulnerable and times when it is not (we discuss this further later in this book). The point to be made here is to understand that in strong school cultures, moving to a virtual island and building a new "structure" is risky. It needs to be a gradual process that does not create a lot of noise. It is better to begin in silence so that the new structure has a chance to become established and more sustainable.

When creating a safe place, we can think of Abraham Maslow's hierarchy of needs (Maslow, 1943) or William Glasser's five basic needs (Glasser, 1998). And remember that this "safe" place exists in our head. Whereas some cultures may stake physical territory in certain places in the school building (e.g., a workroom, tables at faculty meetings, parking spaces), that is not where we go first. The safe place we need is more about efficacy and permission to experiment than it is about marking our territory.

In schools, teachers are the main repositories of the culture. Each teacher has a personality that contributes more or less to the strength of that culture. Some are very influential and some are hardly noticed. Other adults in the building, such as support staff, may also be influential in terms of affecting daily operations and the mood of the group. With these elements in mind, we suggest that you try the following activity. (Note that this is something to do on your own, as it could generate misunderstandings or resentment among people in your building.)

Write the names of your teachers and staff members on different-colored sticky notes and place them on the matrix shown in Figure 3.1, arranging them relative to the degree of influence each has on the school's current culture. The ones on the bottom (9s and 10s) are the foundation and represent the strongest personalities. It is important to note that they may be effective or ineffective as teachers or staff; what you are considering is their level of influence. Teachers or staff who seem to go unnoticed or lack influence may be 1s or 2s. Let the colors represent effectiveness, such as blue for the most effective, yellow for the somewhat effective, and red for the ineffective. You should end up with many blues in the bottom half of the matrix if your school culture is an effective one. Creating a depiction such as this can give you a sense of how the culture is made up of its members and a strong visual of what your culture is like when you sum up the parts.

Now create a second matrix, one that represents the culture you want. Position the people you want as the foundation of the new culture, even if their personalities are not yet strong, and place the ones you don't need either on the top or on an island.

Looking at the two matrices (current and desired), you can see who the main players are, who you need to have available to set the foundation, and who you need to be unnoticeable (or gone). If you used red, yellow, and blue sticky notes, the idea is to get more blues in the lower half and more reds in the upper half. So, who do you move first, and what does that really look like?

A Matrix to Show Levels of Influence of Teachers and Staff

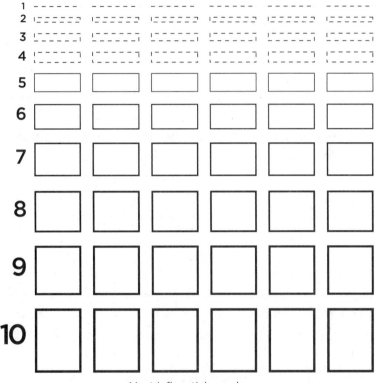

Least influential people

Most influential people

Culture relies on peer pressure, so you need to use peers to pressure others to move. If you have some blues on the bottom row, start there. Are any of them able to carry your vision or ideas to a few other blues who may be near the middle or top? Keep in mind that your goal is not a mass exodus. You need only a few who are willing to make an effort to hang together as they experiment with some new ideas. If this sounds simplistic, it is, but remember, you need to provide the safe zone as others begin to sense strange behaviors in familiar places.

Now you can begin to understand how the right *people can improve a culture.* It is possible that your current culture is quite effective but could use some tweaking. If you struggled to create a desired culture that was much different from the current culture, then you may already have what you need and this activity is an indicator suggesting you should not mess with it too much.

However, much of this chapter and the sticky-note exercise are based on the premise that the current culture is ineffective; thus the culture you want may need to start out as an island. The first people to inhabit this island are critical to its proper development. This is our way of making a complex network of personalities easier to grasp. The path between the culture and the island is laid with new norms, routines, and stories, as well as a new climate.

Once the island begins to reach critical mass, the culture there will become a resource for improving people—namely, the rest of the faculty and staff. Now the pathway becomes a superhighway, going one way only. *The culture is being used to improve people.*

This process is not about telling people what to do; it is more about praising teachers when they do something great and reminding the others what they could do. It is about creating the conditions for people to improve by using peer pressure and creating safe zones. It is about making the effective teachers into the cool teachers.

As a leader you must also be aware that because culture exists in our minds, you need to help new staff members see the island as the preferred culture within the school. By adding new staff members and encouraging other positive staff to relocate there, you are building a subculture. If you continue this process, the new subculture can actually become the culture.

What if you only want to tweak the culture rather than have a major shift? When teachers leave and you have openings in your matrix, you want to make sure your new teachers can become a part of the foundation, moving others to a higher and less influential point on the cultural matrix. If you hire less effective teachers, you are just adding new staff to the top rows, slowing the growth of the desired culture.

Keep in mind that the very best people in a less-than-positive culture are already looking for cracks. They are closest to the door or window in the culture. If you as a leader do not provide them a safe place to relocate to, they may find one in another school—or worse, in another profession. Leaders have to be aware that everyone is not equal in terms of effectiveness and that being aware of this is a critical component of being able to alter the culture by adjusting the makeup or location of the people in it.

The same is true in a positive culture. The most negative people are continually looking for a way out because they are not surrounded by, or supported by, other negative people. Thus their opinions are shared in an echo chamber at first and then eventually are not shared at all. To feel comfortable, they have to find a place where *how they feel and think* is the norm of the culture—or at least of a subculture. Remember, everyone wants to fit in. We start by searching locally, and if we cannot find like-minded colleagues quickly, we start to look elsewhere. This is not inherently good or bad. It just is.

When districts look at teacher turnover and departure on a school-by-school basis, they realize that it is not just the number of people relocating that matters; it is the quality of the departing educators that helps to determine whether leaders are guiding the culture in a positive way. And keep in mind that the very best people have more opportunity to switch schools or professions simply because their skill sets are so valued. Effective organizations are seeking people like that. Our struggling peers and colleagues are often dug in regardless of their misery simply because they have fewer alternatives.

As you reflect on your own organization, leadership, and culture, consider which people have left and which ones are itching to get out. That will help you determine if you are intentionally building the type of culture you want for your students and staff.

/ / / / / / /

Now that you know how to lay a foundation for developing the culture you desire, you need to understand how it can assist in improving people and teaching. These are the topics of the next two chapters.

CHAPTER 4

Harnessing
Culture to
Energize and
Enrich People

Reminding teachers that they are part of a great school that has a positive effect on students every day can be very reassuring and empowering.

I n the previous chapter we began our discussion of using people to improve culture and using culture to improve people. Here we look more closely at the latter topic, including the potentially positive role that peer pressure can play. One of our goals in this chapter is to help you as a school leader to recognize opportunities to reduce stress in the lives of teachers rather than try to manage around it. We are not talking about the tough decisions or crucial conversations but rather the subtle moves of a knight in a game of chess. We hope to help you make changes in your schools with humility that characterizes "Level-5 Leadership" (Collins, 2001), and the disposition of a master chess player, as well as to take action without establishing a legacy. If people remember the leader more than the changes, the changes are likely to have a short shelf life when the leadership changes.

One thing to remember is that although we mentioned reducing teachers' stress, that concept is not universally applicable. Perhaps the goal in many circumstances is to selectively reduce most people's stress level. However, it is possible that we need to increase discomfort at certain times for some individuals. If something is too easy, we may not feel any challenge in attempting to do it or any reward once it is accomplished.

How to Use Stress Constructively

Recently we were part of a discussion to help prepare future school–leader interns to be successful on a national exam for principals. One member of our group told the interns that the goal was to eliminate all their stress. This statement struck us as a generalization that does not benefit all future test-takers. Do we really want them to have *no* level of concern? In many groups and schools, don't we see people with too much anxiety and others with too little? Being more selective is a better approach to improving the people in schools.

Sometimes people tend to be less effective if they feel stress or pressure; others respond more positively to stress. Obviously we all have a breaking point at which we feel overwhelmed and become less effective. But there are others who avoid responsibility and do not seem to contribute their fair share to solving stressful situations. Typically these people have learned what to do so that they don't have to do anything. And the culture of the school may be rewarding them for acting this way. In fact, we are certain that the current culture needs them to avoid stress.

Taking a selective approach

Rather than reducing stress on everyone equally, we recommend taking a more selective approach that redistributes concern, diminishing it among those who do a disproportionate amount of work and increasing it among those who seem to avoid any part of the load. This approach will be new to the culture, leading to an uncomfortable changing of roles for some people.

Most, if not all, states have issued myriad new mandates and directives that schools must incorporate into their practices, including new teacher-evaluation models, increased levels of testing and accountability, changes in grading policies, and differentiated pay-per-performance approaches. Some states have focused on a few of these, but many have adopted the smorgasbord of new requirements. This rapid evolution of expectations can cause a swirl of confusion and stress for everyone involved. If the stress lasts a long time, the culture of the school will cause teachers to go into defense mode. As a school leader, you may feel an instinctual protectiveness that seeks to shield and build a protective cocoon around everyone in your school and district. However, we again ask, do we really want to reduce or eliminate this discomfort for *everyone*?

You can help protect the vast majority of caring and dedicated teachers by assuring them that regardless of what the new mandates are, everything will work out. You can share that you do not yet know all the details on this new local, state, or federal directive, but you will make sure it will all be OK, no matter what is involved. Most educators already work hard and expend incredibly energy on their jobs every day. If they feel even more pressure, they may shut down or distance themselves emotionally from the students or the school. This kind of reaction comes with a great cost that has nothing to do with dollars. It is the cost of losing the kind of care that you want teachers to convey to their students. Reminding teachers that they are part of a great school that has a positive effect on students every day can be very reassuring and empowering. Rather than creating a bunker mentality, it can actually enable people to invest more and to have a greater influence on each student.

At the same time, many organizations have a few individuals who either do not work at maximum capacity or their maximum capacity is so limited that they are not effective in their roles. Many schools have a few teachers like this, and we bet a few come to mind as you read this. Chances are they have been at your school a long time—we doubt that a new teacher is trying to get by with minimal effort.

Your goal should not be to decrease anyone's level of concern and effort. For those whose current work ethic and skill level are not at least at a minimal standard, you must ramp up their concern rather than decrease it even more. When such individuals bring up the topic of a new mandate, you can ask, "How are you going to deal with these increased expectations?" or "You must feel like you are going to have to spend your entire summer preparing for all of these changes." You might be tempted to think that having these slugs uninvolved actually helps the school move forward. Although it may seem appealing to have the losers go home while you plan your next moves, doing so will promote an undercurrent of frustration among the effective teachers. They are watching. So, let the ineffective teachers feel the stress.

The dedicated and caring majority of teachers already spend an incredible amount of their personal time, their summer vacation, and their weekends thinking about school, and many wrestle with issues such as how to reach the seemingly unreachable students. Helping to lower their level of concern can be beneficial to their mental health and morale and may reduce potential future burnout. But it is important to remember that one of the reasons they are so effective is because they *do* think a lot about how they can have a more positive influence on students. The culture must value these people, which means an informal support group will develop whether you are orchestrating it or not.

With this in mind, isn't the goal to try to help your less effective and dedicated staff members actually become more like their more dedicated peers? Increasing their emotional and mental buy-in can enable those who do not often reflect on their students and their own performance to become more like those who do. You cannot make them care, but you can make it cool to care. Remember that this will be a role change for them. Let them enjoy small wins when they seem to start caring and sharing.

Eustress—The healthy stress

Rather than thinking about how to minimize stress within your organization, perhaps you should focus on redistributing *eustress* within your school. *Eustress* is the type of stress that is healthy. If the majority of dedicated people feel free to do the right thing and the others who seem less invested feel more pressure to do the right thing, it can actually create a world in which the students end up benefiting the most. Thinking about your school and district, can you picture those who would be more productive if you reduced their responsibilities and concerns, and others who would increase their efforts if the opposite occurred?

Recall your favorite movie. Chances are the actors in that movie did a great job, and the script, the roles, and the directing all came together. Many times great movies have sequels with the same people playing the same roles. Imagine any sequel with actors changing roles in future movies from the series. People will get upset if they find their favorite actor in a different role (especially in the sequel). Imagine anyone other than Michael J. Fox playing Marty McFly in the *Back to the Future* series! Teachers also become type-cast into roles, but this may not be a good thing; they can become stuck in a role. Reducing or increasing responsibilities, or expectations, for anyone on staff who has been there a long time will make some people upset. Everyone knows what movie they are in and who is playing what role. If you want to change any part of your school's movie, your staff will need some time to adjust. If anyone other than Daniel Radcliffe tries to play Harry Potter, your staff may not care about how well everything else is put together (more on this later).

The Power of Peer Pressure

Here is another way to look at how a group can affect the individual's performance. Many of us can recall doing group work when we were in school. Although the teacher may have thought she was increasing collaboration and learning, often the high achievers felt like they were being disproportionally "dumped on" because they felt the pressure to do a good job and get an *A*. Others may have welcomed group work because they felt that they did not actually have to do any of the work. Perhaps in some classrooms there were expectations that *did* result in a more collaborative process, with students learning from each other and growing together. But if you ask first-year college students how much they like group work, most will say they hate it.

By using peer pressure, we can make subtle changes in the way teachers collaborate. By developing a culture in which sharing and collaborating are expected, we can have synergistic results. We then can use the school culture to help rebalance the responsibilities in the organization. Taking this approach makes it possible to see how we can use the culture of an organization to improve the people within it.

How Culture Overpowers Diverse Beliefs

One potential value of using groups is to bring diversity of thought into problem solving. Rather than have one person sit alone and attempt to think of solutions, a collaborative culture brings a group of people together to gain multiple perspectives. Culture, however, often kills diversity. The objective of culture is to converge the new people's values and beliefs toward those of its members. Any diverse perspective will need to be modified, if not deleted, so the holder of these beliefs can maintain good standing in the group. This is the "melting pot" effect: the more time I spend with you, the more I become like you. Imagine a midwesterner spending six months in New York City or New Orleans. A speaker of the local dialect will recognize the midwesterner when he first arrives with comments like "You're not from around here, are you?" After a few months, the visitor will begin to take on qualities of the locals to the point that when he returns home he will be confronted with some admonishment about how he speaks. It happens with food, clothing, language, and many other habits of life, as well—even our dispositions toward waiting in line. The visitor or a new person tends to assimilate and become more like those people in the culture surrounding him than he influences the group. Over time, collaboration builds a "group think" mentality.

This is what cultures do. They redefine what it means to be "normal around here." They reward fitting in; they don't care much for outliers. Given this cultural convergence theory, what can you in your school leader role do as you try to improve your school? Is this a dynamic you are stuck with and need to fight, or is there a way you can use available cultural forces to your advantage?

Keep in mind that not all diverse ideas are positive. There are some real crazies out there. Some diverse ideas can enable us to improve, but others can have the opposite effect. Often we assume that a group collectively thinks better than an individual, but this is only true if the group settles on the best decision. A popular contemporary expression says that "The smartest person in the room is the room." This is clever and catchy and may be true. It actually *should* be true, but many times we know that it is not the case.

Reflect on decisions you made when you were in middle school, high school, or college. For example, when you were deciding what to do over the weekend with your friends, did you typically end up choosing the best idea that was tossed out, or did you at times settle on the idea of the person who was the most popular, the best looking, the most athletic, or the only one with a car? We may assume that this is not how things happen among adults, but we can all identify times when the wrong criteria informed the action taken, which may not have led to the best result.

Personalities, group dynamics, subcultures, and cultures can lead us down a predetermined path. This can be good or bad. Depending on who is in the room, when one person starts complaining about the administration or a particular student or parent, the conversation can quickly cease or turn negative. This same phenomenon can result when someone suggests an idea that would benefit students, or the school, but could result in more work for everyone involved. Sometimes the idea is immediately shut down, but at other times it can grow like a musical production in an old Elvis movie.

Have you ever been in a school where if someone asks, "How are you doing today?" and the reply is "Wonderful! How are you?" the happy respondent is greeted with a curt "What are you so happy about?!" Especially if it is Monday? The culture in this setting can help determine which of these two speakers is reflecting the norm of the school. If being happy and perky is not consistent with the way people behave "around here," it is likely that the perky greeter is now rebuked and sent back over to the dark side of public dispositions with his or her peers. However, what if the person who exclaimed, "What are you so happy about?" is met with a smile and others observing then ask, "Are you OK? That seemed so disproportionally rude and negative." If this reaction expresses the cultural norm, it could result in the negative accuser feeling alone and realizing that she needs to have a different response to "fit in" with the culture of the building.

Think about the following events and activities and how your staff usually responds to each of them. Imagine what kind of response you would get from the average teacher in your school if you mentioned the following:

- Faculty meeting
- Professional development
- Snow day
- Testing
- New teachers
- Lunch duty
- PLCs

Now, think about the response you'd get from people in a collaborative and positive school culture. An open, positive, and collaborative culture can be an important tool to use in improving the people in a school. But remember, having a collaborative culture does not solve problems; it provides a framework for problems to be solved, rather than letting a situation fester into something big later on. Furthermore, you do not have to wait—and cannot afford to wait—until the collaborative culture is completely established and refined. If improving the people in a school does not occur simultaneously with developing a positive culture, the culture can never become what you would like it to be. Improving a culture and improving people are two processes that move in conjunction with each other. One may advance at a different pace than the other, but they will parallel each other in growth. In cultures, people watch each other and try to determine what is "normal," and then they try to act accordingly. If you do not move most staff members forward simultaneously, then you typically move none of them forward.

The Role of Leaders: Establishing Norms and Serving as a Conscience

Leaders can and do play a major role in establishing the norms in an organization. When you were little, you probably often heard voices of your parents, teachers, or others saying things like "Don't steal" or "Lying is wrong." Eventually—we hope— the voices of others were replaced by your own conscience telling you what was right or wrong. Rather than hearing a subconscious reminder not to steal that pack of gum, you just knew that was something you would not do. This seems like common sense and inherent in everyone. But at times we may have differing views of what is right and wrong. How we treat students can come from the wisdom of many different sources.

Many of us had part-time jobs when we were in high school or college. Although for most of us it may have been a temporary position, we often worked alongside others who were in a permanent position in their career or profession. One of us (Todd) had a job while in college, working at a very nice restaurant as a waiter. His instinct is to be on time (or even early to make sure he's not late), work as hard as he can, and not be a complainer. He had always assumed everyone else had the same beliefs and practices. At the restaurant he showed up promptly for his Friday evening shift, which was a great time slot because the eatery would be busy and tips would be lucrative. Two of the other servers were not there at 5 p.m., when the shift began. It didn't matter at first because there were not that many customers at that early hour. But gradually the place would become packed, and even if it were fully staffed, the pace would be frenetic. With some people missing, it really became wild. Eventually he asked what happened to the two no-shows.

Turns out they were often erratic in their attendance, and no one even thought it was strange. Night after night during the summer, Todd would show up on time, not knowing how many others would be working alongside him. Some would come an hour or so late, and others never arrived. He remembers thinking how weird it was that people felt no obligation to call in and didn't apologize when they finally did arrive, even though the job was their livelihood. But then what really struck him was a realization that it seemed no one else thought it was unusual. It was actually "normal" to have people not come to work. Not only did their peers seem oblivious to it, the restaurant managers thought that this was just standard operating procedure. The culture of the organization matched the expectations of the leaders. Todd rationalized this situation, assuming this must be what it is like in a non-professional environment. He thought to himself, "Of course, it would never be like this in a school full of dedicated and caring educators."

Then when he became a teacher, he noticed that colleagues would call in sick because they were tired or wanted to go shopping. They would have a 30-minute dentist appointment at 9:00 a.m. and miss the entire day. Of course, not everyone would do this, but it seemed like a large enough group that it became the norm of the school.

What was also obvious was that the people who felt the most comfortable doing things like this—cutting corners, telling white lies, and so on—tended to associate with others who would do similar things and then rationalize why it was OK. They would say things like, "The meeting yesterday went 'til 4:15 and they only pay us until 4." What had happened was that early in their careers they had interacted with other people who validated these seemingly inappropriate behaviors. They formed their own subgroup (a support group of sorts), which eventually created its own subculture. It is important to know that people will identify with a subculture more than the school's culture if it is strong enough. What a newcomer would clearly consider to be wrong and inappropriate becomes acceptable or even expected, because that is what the person sees so many others doing.

This same thing can happen with complaining. Many people do not like to complain. It makes them feel unhappy, down, or even ugly. However, their desire not to complain means they also do not want to complain about, or especially confront, others who do complain. Thus what often happens is that we only hear complainers, because noncomplainers are much less likely to express their own views. They are reluctant to do so because either (1) that can seem like complaining, or (2) the complainers turn their aggressions toward the noncomplainers instead of what it was they were previous griping about. Remember, the culture will often support complainers who have been a part of that culture for a long time. That is how the organization's culture "solves" problems. It lets the complainers do their thing.

We all know individuals who tend to be darkly negative. Others inspire us to be on our best behavior when we are around them. These two types of people can be in the same workplace or even in the same family. Our own expectations and behaviors shift, depending on who we are interacting with. In these cases we are the malleable ones. We may even know that letting ourselves be pulled toward a negative outlook is wrong, and yet the culture's negativity is stronger than we are. Our inner voices and sense of right or wrong get recalibrated because of the people we associate with most frequently and the culture that rewards certain behaviors.

One of the major responsibilities of leaders is to be the conscience for people who may waiver or even lack a conscience. Leaders need to continually model what is right, but doing so is never enough. Most people cannot learn only from role models. The reason is simple: Every organization has both positive and negative role models. If we do not help guide people to understand and follow the positive models, many will head down the other path.

Many parents can get their children to behave when they are looking, but some have the ability to develop children who will do the right things when they are not being observed or when the parent will not know the child's choice. As they grow into young adults, many children start to develop their own inner voice that guides their actions. Others seem not to develop as quickly as we would hope. And others still seem not to have reached that point regardless of their age.

As a school leader, you must assume that the people who work in your school will do the right thing with students even when no one—including you—is looking. Thinking about room locations, planning times, and mentors can help to ensure the best role model is accessible to new faculty. But you must be a consistent guide, aware of the behind-the-scenes interactions that can occur.

////////

It can be difficult for teachers and staff members to resist when a culture pulls them in a negative direction, but you must provide support and guidance to those who are willing to do so. At the same time, you must also be aware that as people begin to do the right thing on a regular basis, that positive direction becomes the culture, and it will help keep everyone on the path toward doing what is best for the students. Newly hired teachers will come into the setting with diverse beliefs. The school's culture will try to get each of them to accept "the way we do things around here." Whenever possible, put the new teachers close to your best teachers.

CHAPTER 5

Using Culture
to Enhance
Teaching

How can your school move from sympathy to empathy—from whining to brainstorming?

When we talk about using the culture to improve people, one of our biggest aims is to improve the teaching that occurs in each classroom. This part of the book looks at the culture of the school as a catalyst to improve how teachers teach. Keep in mind that improving the culture does not improve the school; it only makes improvement possible. Schools get better when the teachers do a better job of teaching. The culture can allow this to happen—in fact, the culture can demand that it happen. This chapter and the next one look at a few cultural components—collaboration, learning moments, and student voice—that educators may find are more receptive to change than others. We call them cultural leverage points. In Chapter 7 we will examine the *layers* of culture that influence how teachers teach.

It will not shock many of you if we state that the quality of learning depends upon the quality of teaching. Similarly, the quality of teaching depends upon the quality of teachers. No big surprises yet. But what if we suggested that the culture of your school could improve your weak teachers, as well as decrease the effectiveness of your best teachers?

Some may believe they have the strength to overpower their culture—as if they were stronger than the rest of the group combined. But history is full of examples of charismatic leaders coming into a new organization and making big changes only to have the group regress back to "normal" once the person left. With each regression, the group becomes a bit more resistant to the next change. It is the job of culture to provide comfort and predictability to its members. Cultures provide the immune system necessary to ward off the virus of new leadership. Can we use this force to our advantage?

In terms of teaching, we have suggested that the best professional development may come from another teacher in the building, usually in an informal setting. When there is trust, people are more willing to share what *does not* work. It becomes easier to share a lesson that failed whether in the company of another teacher during lunch or at the front of the room during a faculty meeting. By the way, this is probably already happening to some extent in your school, every day. Teachers are sharing ideas and trading tips. They are talking about students, and sometimes the students' parents. They are sharing their frustrations, hoping for solutions. Some of those solutions will work to help students improve. Some will make the teacher's job easier. Some of those solutions will not be helpful to students. Some will amount to acceptance of an attitude that says, "quit caring."

Are there schools where teachers regularly share their professional concerns with each other? How can you as a school leader amplify this process and make it *normal* on a larger scale? How can you allow teachers to safely share the problems they are encountering? How can your school move from sympathy to empathy—from whining to brainstorming? A good place to start is to understand the nuances of collaboration.

Not Everyone Is Created Equal: Collaboration's Effect on the Group

A collaborative school culture uses the expertise of its faculty to solve many of its problems. In these schools, the adults in the building trust each other, and each has an equal voice. Given this democratic approach to problem solving, teachers feel enabled to engage in professional discourse that may occasionally become critical. Listening to feedback from one's peers can be a very valuable experience as teaching strategies are analyzed for effectiveness. However, be careful when a weak teacher attempts to influence a strong teacher. When teachers collaborate, it can be a challenge to screen out bad ideas.

Is it ever possible for the strength of a teacher's personality to create the illusion of competence? Is the smartest person in the room the one who talks the most? Do your best teachers cringe when weak teachers profess weak methods—only to remain quiet (polite) so as not to hurt others' feelings? All teachers are not created equal. They do not have similar K–12 experiences, nor do they complete their preparation programs at the same levels; and most of all, some will be influenced by the current school culture more than others.

Sometimes newly hired teachers bring with them skills and attributes that can have a positive influence on the existing school culture. If you want your school to absorb more of the new teachers' attributes, then you need to find a way to let their voices be heard despite the ambient noise of the culture. To do this, you will need to recognize when a new idea is being proposed and when an old belief is trying to kill it. Not everything a new teacher says will be profound; unfortunately, in some schools anything a new teacher says will be discounted. Most schools have veteran teachers who feel they have been successful. They use their past success to leverage the present. In their view, new teachers were not part of the experiences of this school's staff and thus do not have the (local) perceived expertise necessary to be successful in the future (which also means they have not had to endure the many battles that veteran teachers have fought—and proudly won—to get to where they are now).

That is the foundation of cultural strength: New teachers must learn "the way we do things around here" to be validated by the veterans. Being validated is a form of respect, but being *validated* does not always mean being *effective*.

Imagine working with a group of faculty and staff, each having different experiences, capacities, and expertise. They are given a problem to solve. In this situation, have you ever experienced the following?

- Some will try to make the new problem resemble a past problem and apply past practice (hammer-to-nail theory).
- Some will try to make it seem like the sky is falling.
- Some will try to blow it off as another storm that will soon pass.
- Some will bloviate their solution in a loud and in-your-face manner, daring anyone to challenge it.
- The introverts will be quiet.
- The smartest person in the group may not engage.

It is possible that when some groups collaborate, the best solutions are never put on the table. Why does this happen, and how can you harness available energy to engineer the best from a group? It would not be productive to have a "collaborative" culture that allows only certain people to speak on script, all the time. Some of the best ideas may sound pretty crazy at first, and unfortunately some school cultures will not let crazy ideas be shared. In some schools, collaboration is a way to perpetuate the past: "Let's make sure we are all on the same page" can be considered a form of collaboration but it is really just group think.

What would a school look like if every idea had a chance to be heard publicly without fear of judgment? What if every teacher were asked to bring new ideas to each meeting? What if bringing new ideas were the norm and those who did not were made to feel bad? You can use peer pressure to influence teachers to think about new approaches to teaching, to record those ideas, and to share them with others. Engineering how you collaborate can be a leverage point for changing a culture.

Think about faculty meetings and how the culture plays out in that setting. Each person already has a role and script—you know what each person will do and say. So, use this to create a better meeting. Here's a typical agenda:

1. Welcome
2. Success stories
3. Classroom management
4. Parent involvement
5. Student assessment
6. Challenges
7. Open conversation

Is there a way you could arrange the room and place individuals strategically in order to have a more effective meeting? How might your knowledge of the current culture be used to make this happen? If you know the roles (and scripts) of each faculty member, can you build a play (as in theater) based on those characters and create a drama that engages their passions? Or can you build a play (as in football) to take advantage of your culture's strengths? Many times generals in battle and coaches on the football field will think about what the other side has done in the past to try to predict their next move. Knowing their next move is an advantage. If the culture in your school is strong, you know its next move. Come to your next faculty meeting knowing how people will react. Let those who have success on the agenda item have the loudest voice.

Protecting the Moment of Learning

There is a moment when we learn something. This moment may happen in classrooms, while we are driving, while we are having lunch, or during a performance. Teachers live for this moment with their students.

Similarly, there is a moment in time when we realize we have improved. From that moment on, we will be in a different place mentally, our confidence will be stronger, our self-esteem may increase, and our capacity to do more will drift into our awareness. This moment is also a time when an old belief may be vulnerable to a new belief, or vice versa. This personal moment of learning needs to be protected from old beliefs.

This process is essentially the same for schools. It takes time for schools to improve. We can prove that a school has improved through the use of many forms of data. The question we are asking here is, exactly when did improvement occur? Is there a tipping point? To some, these questions may seem irrelevant; they may say, "As long as a school improves, who cares when it actually happens?" Our contention is that if we are able to identify that moment, then we need to protect it—just as we would "protect" a student's new learning. We wonder how many schools get very close to this moment only to have it sabotaged or compromised because we were unable to be quiet and let it happen, or an old belief overshadowed it just as it was about to take root.

This thought came to us during a recent professional development event for teachers and administrators. The speaker was providing a great amount of good information and delivering it in a way that made sense. The audience members were taking it all in, engaged in thought as he spoke and mentally applying the information to their local setting. Some were jotting down notes, some were leaning over sharing ideas with their neighbors, and some were simply mesmerized by the speaker's passion.

What happened next was what caused us to look at each other and then drop our heads. The speaker gave the audience time to process what he was sharing *for only three minutes*, reminding the crowd at the two-minute mark and then at the one-minute mark. So he actually gave us two very short sessions to process potential breakthroughs in thinking about our schools. This happened many times over the course of three hours. Many times the audience members were brought to a point of total engagement in processing our individual schools' future only to have those thoughts derailed by an artificial time limit. Is it possible that many schools represented at this event were at the edge of improving, about to experience a tipping point, only to be sabotaged by one person's need to get through the presentation?

Let's take a look at what a school might do to improve. As you work with your leadership team or with your faculty, think about whether there are crucial moments for learning to occur. Looking at the list below, determine the *moment* this school improved:

- Leaders/teachers go about normal business at school.
- Information is provided (e.g., student complaints, media reports, parent concerns), implying the school's performance is inferior.
- Leaders think about this information and share their feelings with teachers.
- Data are collected relevant to the information.
- Data are reviewed and analyzed by leaders.
- Data are reviewed and analyzed by teachers.
- Plans are made to address the areas of concern.
- Professional development is provided to support deployment of the plans.
- The plans are deployed; we experience the new stuff.
- Deployment is discussed.
- New data are collected after a period of time to verify if plans are working.

So, at what *moment* did the school improve? Perhaps each moment contributed to learning in varying degrees. Most important, is there a way to protect the moment(s) of improvement from sabotage? We believe the culture of your school knows when these moments are about to occur and will find ways to derail the improvement. The derailing may simply be a veteran teacher rolling her eyes, or it may be a parent expressing disapproval of proposed changes at a school board meeting.

This reminds Todd of a time when critics of his leadership believed that he was in his office too much, that he needed to get out and wander more. They were right. So he wandered. And each time he was welcomed with a strange look. One person even commented, "What are you doing here?"

As this anecdote illustrates, it is possible the critics will not support your new behavior even though they recommended it. Over time you will develop a role that has a script. If that script calls for you to be in your office much of the day, going off script will not be received well if it creates imbalance or confusion in the culture, even if it could improve the school.

So What?

First, could we use this kind of analysis in the classroom? Is there a moment when a student is close to understanding a complex concept only to be derailed by the teacher's need to move on?

As a new idea drifts from phases of vulnerability to a new belief, some cultures have been waiting for these final moments of doubt, hoping to ambush it. If *you* don't know when the culture is about to learn (change) something, we are sure it—the culture—does. These are the times when the culture does its thing—it protects people by reminding them of what was successful in the past when they are about to step into a dark, unfamiliar place. This is not a nefarious act; it is simply a means for survival. Listen for the voices in the crowd as something new is presented, especially when the topic is something as personal as teaching. You know it is coming.

///////

Teacher evaluation has long been one way to attempt to improve teaching performance in the classroom. It has undergone dramatic changes in many places recently as it has been tied to performance pay with test scores as one component. In the next chapter we look at how incorporating student voices into teacher evaluation might play a key role in the culture–people dynamic.

CHAPTER 6

Empowering
Student Voices

Student voices are powerful factors in teacher professional development.

As currently structured, education gives principals the primary responsibility for the quality of teaching that occurs in their buildings. Each principal is armed with a teacher evaluation process that may include everything needed: rules of observations, rubrics to distinguish the effective from the ineffective, deadlines, remediation protocols, and scripts to use when giving feedback. Additionally, many places use test scores as a component of teacher evaluation, and some use teacher evaluation as a tool that affects pay and employee retention.

The culture of education is such that some school leaders use these processes to improve teacher effectiveness and some may use it to exact revenge. Some may see it as a distraction, whereas some may see it as an opportunity to talk about improvement. Regardless of what the main purpose of teacher evaluation may be on paper, the culture will determine what it means and how valuable it will be. And, though students are the ones living through the consequences, rarely do we find the students' voices as part of the teacher evaluation process.

Viewing Student Engagement and Instruction Through a Different Lens

Here's a culture buster: Embrace diverse feedback from informed sources. The purpose of this chapter is to give you ideas for how to work with teachers to see their practice through a different lens: a lens provided by their students. Help teachers see their own craft through their students' eyes by asking students for their take on some of the following critical aspects of effective student engagement and instruction.

Creating safe, welcoming, and exciting learning environments. As a critical first step before anything else can get better, teachers must know if students feel safe in their class. But an optimal learning environment must go far beyond that determination. Encourage teachers to also find out from their students if their learning environment engages them in the learning process. For example, do students consider their classroom a *great* place to learn? Do the students get to engage with the wider world beyond the classroom in their learning? When was the last time they stepped out of the classroom—or out of the school or the local community—as part of their lesson? Questions like these will help paint a clear picture of how well a teacher creates a great space for meaningful learning.

Making learning fun, interesting, and relevant. Effective engagement is essential for student learning, so work with teachers to find out how much students like being in their class. The only way to find this out is to put a few questions to the students: Does the subject matter make sense? Is it interesting and relevant to students' interests and priorities, inside and outside of class? Does the teacher get excited about the material and help students get excited as well? How much fun is it to be in the class? Answers to these kinds of questions will help teachers gauge just how much their approach is connecting with students.

Doing what it takes to ensure that all students work through any challenges to achieve mastery. Helping kids embrace the struggles and occasional failures in their learning trajectory is one of the biggest challenges teachers face, but it is also a big opportunity for them to help students understand how invested their teachers are in their success. Help teachers learn more about students' feelings on how much they think the teacher strives to make sure all students learn. Does the teacher work with struggling students, trying different approaches and various resources to help them grasp and master the subject matter? Do students feel prepared when it's time to test their knowledge? Does the teacher follow up with students after a test, explaining the results in a way that leaves the students feeling encouraged and ready to tackle upcoming goals in the class? Understanding students' feelings on these issues will help teachers better determine if students believe that their teacher is on their side.

Challenging students to push their thinking and take ownership of their learning. It's not enough just to help students through the rough spots. Students also need to sense that teachers want them to take their thinking to the next level. Do students feel that the teacher pushes them to reflect and think critically about what they're learning and articulate those thoughts in class as part of the learning process? Collaborate with teachers on ways to find out how—or even *if*—their students see this happening in their class.

Making sure students know that they are seen and heard, respected, and valued. This aspect may be the most important of all, after student safety. Students must feel that they matter, and teachers must be confident that every student feels that way. You can remind teachers that students need to feel respected and valued. The following questions can help teachers assess their status. Do students feel that their ideas and opinions matter to the teacher? Does the teacher encourage them to open up and share aspects of their personal lives? Do they get the sense that the teacher likes every student? Does the teacher deal with problems, such as student misbehavior, fairly and appropriately? How do parents seem to feel about the teacher? Do students sense that the teacher is comfortable with their parents? Do they think their parents feel like welcome partners in their child's learning? Answers to questions like these will shed light on how valued students feel as equal members of a class community.

This is a formative approach to teacher improvement. There should be opportunities to experiment with new ways to teach, new ways to interact with students, and perhaps a new mindset. Using an action research model can help supply these new ideas. We are developing an evidence-based teacher effectiveness inventory, which explores these questions using a scientific, systematic data collection and reporting approach. We expect it will serve as a powerful tool to help teachers discover strengths to build on and weaknesses to address.

How School Culture Affects Reactions to Student Input

If the culture of your school is a collaborative one, teachers will find it natural to exchange thoughts about student input. Whether they share their strengths or weaknesses, the outcome of these conversations will be helpful and ongoing. If you do not have a collaborative school culture, it will soon be obvious that the effort to collect student input was wasted time and it really has no basis to inform teacher effectiveness, let alone teacher evaluations.

Individual teachers will vary in how much they self-reflect on results from any source. Some will alter their practices and continually reassess to see if there is improvement. Others will more likely rationalize the responses away. Self-talk such as "what do these kids know about effective teaching" or "they never take things like this seriously" can easily occur in almost all settings. Much of the reaction depends on the culture of a school. If the norm is not to use opportunities like this to grow, then naysayers will have plenty of supporters providing built-in excuses.

In a more collaborative setting where there is sharing, what will quickly become evident is the vast difference between and among teachers in the same school, grade level, and subject area. What is also obvious is that different people have varying strengths and weaknesses. A safe and protected school environment makes it possible to take advantage of this disclosure, reinforcing the idea that the culture allows and possibly even expects growth and development. It is also important that leaders not discount the potential benefit of outlier teachers self-reflecting, even if they do so in a vacuum. We must not allow the negativity of a few to prevent us from doing something that will benefit the biggest risk takers and those most focused on personal growth. The outliers should not be called out as examples and embarrassed, but they should also not be prevented from asking these important questions of students even if the answers will benefit only themselves.

/ / / / / / /

Despite teacher evaluations being a traditional professional responsibility of the principal, student voices are powerful factors in teacher professional development. A few students may not take this process seriously, but doesn't that happen among teachers, too? There are many ways to determine teacher effectiveness, and there are many layers in a school that influence their effectiveness. The next chapter explains those layers.

CHAPTER 7

Understanding the Layers of Culture

Any reference to a culture "of" something tells us that the speaker does not truly understand what a culture is.

As we have noted, any culture is a subculture of a larger culture. But there is not a culture for everything. Some practices may be common or understood without written rules, but that does not mean they constitute a culture.

For example, when applauding the success of someone, the audience members may begin to stand as they clap. This standing ovation is like a wave we see at baseball games—nobody wants to be seen sitting down when everyone else is standing. Even if some people in the audience roll their eyes when they see others start to stand and clap, the social pressure to do so is usually overwhelming, and so everyone eventually stands and claps. This is a common practice at many award ceremonies. It is not written down as a rule and there is no "culture" of award ceremonies.

Similarly, people tend to drive at the speed that other drivers are going, staying with the flow rather than adhering strictly to the posted speed limit. In many situations, such as on certain highways, the unwritten rule is to drive 65 to 75 miles per hour when the posted speed limit is 55 miles per hour. It may actually be unsafe to drive 55 miles per hour. In this situation there is a social expectation to fit in; each road has anticipated traffic patterns, but that does not mean there is a "culture" of traffic.

When we hear about people trying to create a culture of assessment, of trust, or of learning, what we think they mean is a culture that embraces assessment, trust, and learning. A separate culture need not—does not—exist for each component we are trying to develop (Edgar Schein, personal communication, April 28, 2016). We have had the opportunity to speak at various conventions and listen to presentations from others. We gravitate toward those who include the words "school culture" in their titles. It is annoying when speakers are encouraging others to build cultures of assessment, cultures of learning, cultures of trust, and so on, as if there were hundreds of cultures out there and perhaps hundreds more to be created. Any reference to a culture "of" something tells us that the speaker does not truly understand what a culture is.

Schools have *one culture* (with subcultures), and this one culture tells members how to respond to assessment, learning, or trust. It is not as if leaders could create a culture of assessment; rather, leaders need to shape the current culture to embrace assessment. To believe you need to create so many 'cultures'— each one focusing on an individual component that exists within a school culture—cheapens the overall construct. To us, to create a culture of assessment is akin to creating a religion that worships food. After studying culture for many years, we feel the need to protect it from those who don't understand it.

To claim there is a classroom culture may be a reach also. Cultures take years to materialize. What happens before the classroom group becomes a culture can be debated, and some will feel like the pressures to assimilate have the force of a culture. Although we could drift into a philosophical argument regarding the properties of true cultures, the point here is not to debate whether a setting is actually a culture, but rather to understand the various layers and how each influences the others.

The Classroom Culture

Assuming for now that there is such a thing as a classroom culture, we can confidently say that the culture is determined by the teacher. Students may have a 2 percent impact on it (Cruz, 2015), but cultures are built by adults. Just as no two schools are alike, no two classrooms are alike. We may have two teachers who are the same race and gender, have the same number of years of experience, who went to the same college, and attend the same church, but have different class cultures. They may even have the same students, but each classroom will feel different, and this difference could become a variable in effectiveness.

Each classroom culture will be influenced by the school's culture, which in turn is influenced by the district's culture. The district's culture will not have as strong an effect as the building's culture, which means the principal will have more influence over what happens in each classroom than the superintendent will. The extent of the principal's influence in each classroom will be determined by the culture of the school. In some schools it is normal for the principal to wander in and engage with the students and the teacher doesn't miss a beat. In other schools the principal will not show up without 48-hour notice, and should the principal decide to show up unexpectedly, some teachers may file a grievance.

Ultimately the teacher decides how the class will respond whenever an administrator enters the room. However, the culture of the school will let that teacher know if the response conforms to the unwritten rules of the system. Returning to our earlier analogy about driving on highways, there is an unposted speed limit for all teachers. To ignore it will bring the teacher some type of punishment, such as teasing, rumors, or shunning. Teachers whose behavior falls into a pattern that goes against the culture can expect to lose their membership in the culture—that is, they may not get the information, security, and feeling of belonging we are all hardwired to need.

The realization that culture can vary dramatically from class to class is significant and can be a helpful impetus toward change. It can be empowering for teachers to become aware of how greatly they influence the culture, regardless of school and district leadership. And it is helpful to principals because they may now know someone in their own school who has "cracked the code" with students and is able to be highly effective regardless of challenges related to students' personal lives and socioeconomic backgrounds. The task at hand is figuring out how to have the most effective teachers become more influential so that they can then influence others and eventually the culture as a whole.

The Building Culture

The culture of a school is built by the adults in the building. It will be influenced by students, parents, and the local community, as well as by district-level staff; however, these influences will be relatively minor because they do not carry the validity of those in the trenches. Call it a "foxhole syndrome." In any school, veteran faculty develop a special membership over time. This membership will transcend teachers' effectiveness (one can be a weak teacher and still belong) as long as they abide by the unwritten rules, including rules that may cover such matters as how to dress as a professional, where to eat lunch, when to speak up at faculty meetings, how to treat special education students, or where to park. These rules set the mood and influence just about everything that happens at a school. The building culture will have the strongest influence of all the layers of culture.

When people speak in general terms about "school culture," most of them are referring to this level, or layer, of culture. Every school's culture is unique, composed of a certain group of people who are in close physical proximity for a long period of time. As we have stated before, in any organization the unwritten rules will help members navigate the social structure. Each adult will adopt a role so that whatever he or she does next will be fairly predictable. In schools, the faculty will gradually take on the personality of the principal, good or bad, strong or weak, caring or not (Fullan & Quinn, 2016).

The building culture creates an overarching set of values and beliefs that will filter down to each classroom. Although these beliefs will manifest in each classroom with a unique spin, the essence will remain. The building level of culture is where we can identify cultural typologies—a continuum of best to worst. The basic values and beliefs that undergird the work of each employee create categories by which we can determine to some degree how effective that school may be. In *School Culture Rewired* (Gruenert & Whitaker, 2015), we discussed a variety of school culture types. In this book we go beyond the descriptions and share not only how the school influences the classroom cultures, but how the classroom cultures might influence the school's culture.

Becoming aware of what the culture is in a school and understanding which people in the school are the most influential is essential so that we can begin to move both the culture and the people in a positive direction. Typically, this awareness and understanding is a starting point for change and progress.

The District-Level Culture

The district-level culture is the layer that encompasses all schools within a geographic boundary. Some states refer to these entities as corporations or communities. At this level we find people engaged in leadership and management of large-scale operations, sometimes several times removed from the activities in classrooms. Although this level does provide oversight of teacher activities, it does so through the development and enforcement of rules and policies. It tries to set the speed limits. The problem is that unwritten rules always trump written rules. Sometimes we wonder, once an unwritten rule is written down, does it become weaker? If we parse the tacit behaviors of the best teachers and write them down (make them explicit), should we anticipate new unwritten rules to prevail over the newly written rules? Does having to write it down imply it is not being followed and is perhaps not perceived as useful?

It might be fun to analyze policies found in a teacher or student handbook and rank items according to the degree to which each is followed to the letter of the law. In your school, which of the following are strictly sacred and which ones are just suggestions?

- Attending faculty meetings
- Dressing professionally
- Sending misbehaving students to the office
- Leaving plans for substitute teachers
- Timing for arrival at school
- Calling parents

Often it helps people at the school level to understand the dynamic (politics) at the district level in order to position themselves for professional growth. If a school can begin to be seen as the favored school by district administrators, it may garner more resources. However, if it becomes the "pet" school, it may pay a price in terms of how it is viewed by other schools and school leaders within the district. Effective school leaders can help position their school in such a way that it can most benefit from the people and resources at the central office level, or at least minimize the negative perspective and resulting harm if it is seen as a less successful setting.

The Need for Collaboration in Challenging Settings

Whether you are considering the classroom, school, or district culture, collaboration and connection among staff plays an important role. For example, it's well known that in every school, some teachers are more successful than others. This reality is actually more obvious in a low socioeconomic status school. In a high socioeconomic status school, most of the students are high achievers on standardized tests and other similar measures, regardless of teacher effectiveness. Even students in the least capable teacher's classroom do pretty well compared with less economically fortunate peers. But in schools where the students have more challenging backgrounds, the gap in student results between the best teacher and the least effective teacher can be much wider. This difference is one reason that struggling schools have the greatest need for collaboration. Because a few people in the school have had greater than expected success, we have to find ways to build connectedness and trust so that the knowledge of a few can become the knowledge of many.

One way that many schools seek to build connectedness and trust is through professional learning communities (PLCs). As Hargreaves (2015) notes,

> The days when individual teachers could just do anything they liked, good or bad, right or wrong, are numbered, and in many places, now obsolete. Teaching is a profession with shared purposes, collective responsibility and mutual learning. But the new expectation that professional cultures have to be ones of collective autonomy, transparency and responsibility, that have to be deliberately arranged and structured around these principles, should not be a license for administrative bullying and abuse or enforced contrivance either. When push comes to shove, as it were, professional learning communities are not and should not be professional data communities or professional test score communities. (p. 140)

Yes, PLCs are the current rage (and they are the main topic of Chapter 10). And some schools believe simply having them solves problems. Our contention is that having them is a *means* for solving problems. How people conduct themselves during these times together will reflect the norms of the school culture. If people are not allowed to collaborate away from these meetings, chances are the quality of collaboration during these events is not being maximized.

Forcing people into PLCs, with agendas and minutes taken, will seem more like court proceedings than a time to be transparent about effectiveness. If the culture did not like the idea of PLCs before your school developed them, we bet the culture still does not care much for them and can find ways to keep their influence minimal. If you want to know if teachers like PLCs, ask them not to meet one week and see if anyone cares.

How Cultures Interrelate

Obviously the cultures on all levels communicate and influence each other. However, a leader must be aware of both the positives and the negatives of these connections. At times, if there is a sense of weak or negative central office leadership, a school can rally against this perceived common enemy. The challenge for principals and other building-level leaders is to make it obvious which side of the road they are on. For example, if it is a matter of no one at the school level—teachers and principals—receiving pay increases, this might naturally lend itself toward the principal being viewed as an "insider." If the board of education issues new mandates, the principal may become more influential because it is not her "fault" that this has happened. However, school leadership requires a delicate balance, because being perceived as disloyal by the central office will damage the ability of the building leader to influence future district-level decisions and may open up the school to a higher level of scrutiny compared with other schools in the district.

Just as the teacher subclimate and the student subclimate within a school interact with each other, either by throwing each other off balance or settling at the same level, the same is true with classroom, building, and district cultures as well. If a school has teachers who are not having success, the school will have limited ability to move forward to the degree that it could. In a struggling district, it will be much more difficult for any school to maximize its potential. And, of course, the more individual schools struggle, the bigger the challenge for the district to achieve the success it would like.

Although each area operates individually, they are inevitably interconnected. This is reality, but no one should use the struggles of others as an excuse for not having the greatest possible positive effect. Know what you can most influence and start from there.

/ / / / / /

Many educators are frustrated with changes and mandates they feel are forced upon them. Others lament the seeming lack of concern or skills of students' parents and families. Being aware of these frustrations is one thing. Choosing to focus energy on complaining is another, and doing so is counterproductive. Don't let reasons become excuses. Being aware of the various cultural layers is beneficial, but making sure you spend the majority of your time and energy on the parts you can most influence is essential.

CHAPTER 8

Disrupting the Culture–People Balance

When we talk about disrupting the balance of a culture, we are not talking about people as much as we are talking about the roles available for people to fill.

ultures need balance. To maintain predictability, each person needs to behave according to his or her own internal script. In your school, do one or two people consistently try to be the comic? Is there always a "devil's advocate" who responds to every new idea? Do the same people seem to be the champions of new concepts, living on the fringe of risk taking? Is there someone who seems to oppose everything, as well as a few who agree to everything?

Here is what we mean by balance: If a culture has three weak teachers, then that culture, as it currently exists, may *need* three weak teachers. To maintain its current identity, which has been sanctified through time, the culture has three roles that need to be filled by teachers who are consistently negative, ineffective, or apathetic (or however you decide to define "weak"). If you were able to remove these teachers or if they were to leave voluntarily, understand that the roles may still persist, waiting to be filled according to the existing culture. If the new people you hire to replace these three weak teachers are put into the same positions, situations, schedules, and proximity to others, chances are they will find and fill those roles. Others will expect them to do so, and doing so may be the easiest way for the new members to fit into the organization. We cannot simply kill off Darth Vader and expect the *Star Wars* series to continue. We need to find a new person to take the role of the antagonist.

So when we talk about disrupting the balance of a culture, we are not talking about people as much as we are talking about the roles available for people to fill. A particularly challenging situation arises when the new teacher or principal follows a veteran of, say, 30 years. An imbalance persists until the role is picked up and deployed with respect to the person who was replaced. As an analogy, consider what Roger Moore had to face as he replaced Sean Connery in the role of James Bond. Many of us 007 fans are still mad—unless we like Daniel Craig.

Deal and Kennedy describe various cultural roles in their book *Corporate Cultures* (1982). We have modified those roles to have more meaning in an educational setting. Imagine who might be fulfilling each of these roles in your school:

- Queen: This teacher has the longest tenure at this school and gets whatever he or she wants and influences administrative decisions more than anyone else.

- Joker: This teacher always tries to be funny, whether appropriate.

- Historian: This teacher shares failures so that new ideas cannot be presented or developed with much support.

Now imagine what happens when one of these people retires. A new person is unlikely to absorb any major role very quickly, so the role becomes destabilized and perhaps is vulnerable to change. The culture will try to resolve this destabilization quickly, with veteran teachers perhaps attempting to take on one of these roles or delegating the role to someone. School leaders who choose to ignore this behind-the-scenes transition will miss a great opportunity. This destabilization period is the time either to change the role or perhaps eliminate it by creating a new role.

Identifying the "Stalwarts"

It is difficult for people to resist the pull of colleagues and culture. However, your school may include some people who can do so without losing peer credibility. These people do not fight the culture or try to overpower it; they simply understand the dynamics of organizational behavior. Being aware of who these individuals are and how best to use them is essential. Some people have an inner voice or "true north" that leads them to do the right thing regardless of peer or outside pressure. Your ability as a leader to identify these stalwarts and then regularly and privately reinforce them, and find others to join them, is a crucial element for making progress. As this subgroup gets larger, you can use it to improve other people. Improvement may occur one person at a time, but eventually you have people who can serve as the foundation of the next culture.

Consider the following analogy. Many of us exercise, try to exercise, hope to exercise, know someone who exercises, or have watched an exercise program on TV late at night. We call this a "sliding scale of fitness." Regardless, the vast majority of people would probably like to exercise regularly. We can say it is difficult to do so because of time, other obligations, cost, and so on, but we all know in our hearts that the biggest challenge to exercising is motivation. How can we make ourselves do something that makes us uncomfortable?

Many of us attempt to motivate ourselves by working out with a partner. We tell ourselves that exercising will be more fun, we can pep each other up, and the other person may be better at it than we are, serving as a positive role model. This sounds like a great idea. The challenge, though, comes if we find a partner who does not like to exercise. Now there are two people who can come up with excuses not to exercise. This is the challenge we face when deciding to link up with others. Hopefully, when we find a partner to help us work out, that person will not make it easy to skip a session.

In the same way, the culture (or a subculture) can enable and encourage others to do things they would never do alone (good or bad). A challenge quickly emerges as the naysayers attempt to dissuade others from making or continuing to make progress. Continuing the exercise analogy, running regularly regardless of the weather makes it seem normal for you and your partner to show up and run. Looking back at the anecdote about restaurant employees in Chapter 4, one of the keys to improving the employees' attendance is that the culture must make it "normal" to show up and make it unacceptable and disconcerting to show up only intermittently.

Just as a culture can hold people back, it can also enable them to achieve more than they ever thought possible. But certain things are necessary for this to occur.

Training Faculty to Be Strong, Not Weak

We know that a collaborative culture may make weak teachers stronger, and the best teachers may be weakened by a toxic culture (Gruenert & McDaniel, 2009). These transformations will probably happen even if nobody acknowledges the existence of a culture. If we leave things alone, the culture will tend to drive everyone toward the group's mean. Our challenge to you is to raise that mean and to lower the standard deviation.

Culture and definitions

As we have said before, there are many types of school culture. If we consider the collaborative school culture as the optimal setting, then what might be some of the less-than-optimal alternatives? Identifying various types of school culture may be useful in discussing what we mean. Think about something that happens in schools and how a different type of culture might "define" that activity. As an example, let's look at the notion of helping teachers become better teachers—professional development (PD)—and how it plays out in various kinds of school cultures:

- In a *toxic* school culture, PD might be anything that makes the teacher's job easier.

- In a *fragmented* school culture, PD might be seen as a distraction.

- In a *balkanized* school culture, PD might simply be how you affirm the status quo.

- In a *contrived* school culture, PD might be a mandate.

- In a *comfortable* school culture, PD might be ways to make it easier to do your job (not the same as *toxic*).

- In a *collaborative* school culture, PD might be considered as a 24/7 way of life.

Can you see how the same concept (PD) can have six variations? There may be 100 variations out there. Our argument here is that the culture defines the concept.

In another example, think about how standardized testing may be defined:

- In a *toxic* school culture, testing is the evidence you need to prove that some of your students cannot learn.

- In a *fragmented* school culture, testing is a way for teachers to compete for awards.

- In a *balkanized* school culture, testing is how some subjects are made more important than others.

- In a *contrived* school culture, testing is why you and your colleagues are doing your job.

- In a *comfortable* school culture, testing is a necessary evil, but manageable.

- In a *collaborative* school culture, testing is one of many forms of assessment teachers can use to plan for the future.

These examples make it easy to see how the same thing can mean different things in different schools. The term *effective* can also mean something different in each school. Thus when a school demands that a teacher be effective, the meaning may be referring to something that resembles good teaching from the 1950s. In some schools, *effective* can mean the same thing as being *helpful*. However the school defines *effective*, it will be what new teachers aspire toward.

A study involving hundreds of schools (Turner, 2013) found outliers that had either surpassed or fallen short of predicted test scores by a dramatic and significant margin. These schools were wide-ranging in terms of socioeconomic makeup. Site visits were then conducted to determine the differences between the overperformers and the underperformers. The study identified many differences, but here are two of them:

- How student achievement was defined

- Impetus for change

Schools that had significantly overachieved on their test scores compared with their predicted scores, given the socioeconomic status of their students, defined student achievement as accepting responsibility, developing a love of learning, and being respectful, in addition to test scores and other components. These schools took a very big-picture view of student achievement. They believed that they needed to develop the whole student rather than just having a narrow focus.

Schools that had underachieved on their test scores compared with their predicted scores, given the socioeconomic status of their students, defined student achievement in terms of test scores only. So the only area they chose to concentrate on was actually the one that they struggled with the most. Their culture was so focused on their weakness that teachers had little to look forward to; there was little inspiration to come to work. Nobody liked being there.

Culture and impetus for change

A second difference between the overachieving and underachieving schools was what caused their impetus for change. Schools that had exceeded their expected test scores (based on the socioeconomic status of their students) made changes when they felt they needed to make changes. They had an internal impetus for change. The culture actually made people want to improve.

The changes were not narrowly tied to testing or specifically to teaching and learning. The schools were uncomfortable with the pace of the lunch line, so they made needed alterations. The process for parents to pick up and drop off their children was awkward and inefficient, so the schools tweaked it. The way in which students passed through the hallways between classrooms was not working well, so the schools changed it. Changes like these, as well as to the math curriculum, were continually addressed. Imagine working at a school where, whenever people find something not working, they fix it. In some schools, getting better is not an option; it is expected.

Could you make a list of the little things at your school that you wish could be fixed tomorrow? Would any of these be on the list?

- Bus drop-off and pick-up procedures
- Lunch periods
- Announcements
- Assemblies
- Open house

Spend a few minutes brainstorming those aspects of your school that seem to annoy or frustrate people, and then ask, "If we change it, who would be upset?" In other words, acknowledge the possibility that the reason we do what we do is usually because it is what we have always done in the past. Someone in the past decided it was a good idea, and so it became a routine. Chances are that person is gone and the routine needs to be modified, if not stopped. Ask, who is protecting these things that make our day at school miserable at times? What do those people have to lose if a change is made? Chances are a thousand other school leaders have asked about this issue, some of them have solved it, and some of them check Twitter and other social media sites every day in search of a solution.

Different schools make changes in different ways. Some may have a leadership team or a school site council. Other schools are more leader-centered in their decision making. Some use input gathered at faculty meetings, whereas others operate more informally. The commonality isn't in how they make changes; it is in how they continually make alterations based on an internal impetus. Going back to the overperformers in the study just described, they believed they needed to do something different, so they did it. They did not wait to be directed or for others to mandate a change before it took place. Instead, their culture of continual self-evaluation and improvement encouraged the faculty to share ideas, self-reflect, and be risk takers in their own classrooms, as needed. Sometimes schools like these may get it wrong (everyone makes mistakes), but that is the nature of a collaborative school culture. Risk taking is owned by all. Mistakes are owned by all. Successes are owned by all.

The schools that underperformed made change predominantly under one circumstance: when they were directed to. Such direction may have come in the form of a new state mandate, a change in a federal law, or a directive from the central office or school board. Each change was forced upon them by something or someone outside of the school, perhaps by an agency that had never set foot in the school.

You may feel like you are in a similar situation, like the schools that face countless mandates. It is interesting to note that the first group of schools in the study—the overperformers—also faced mandates and at times had to make changes because of these. However, by making alterations *only* when forced to, the underperforming schools established a tone that discouraged risk taking and that made change almost offensive because it was something someone made them do, not something that they did because it was best for the students and the school.

When this negative tone becomes the pervasive attitude of faculty and staff, some will wait to be told what to do rather than implement changes as needed. This approach also weakens buy-in tremendously because the change is always someone else's idea, and we know that whatever we are directed to do will likely be short-lived because at some point we will be directed to do something else.

Thus the culture of negativity evolves into something that some school personnel learn to accept, sell, and defend. Once we are able to blame others for our lack of success, life gets easier. Over time, the high levels of frustration become the new normal, and teachers will feel like they are going to battle on each school day. They will be proud for surviving, and they will teach new teachers how to survive. They will feel effective. What was once a negative aspect of the school has now become a merit badge.

Self-Reflection as a Step Toward Change

Educators and school leaders must self-reflect to determine how their school defines student achievement, success, and effectiveness. And they will need to examine how change is addressed in their school. If the established culture encourages and reinforces risk taking—even if doing so doesn't always work out as hoped—it can go a long way to developing strong, resilient, and innovative teachers. Keep in mind that one of the essential factors in developing a collaborative school culture is to reinforce the efforts, not to reinforce the results. By encouraging and valuing any new thoughts and practices, we can help develop and strengthen a culture that will lead to innovation. Shepherding a herd to go in a particular direction once it is moving is often much easier than getting it to take that first step. Coaches who can get their team to play as hard as it can against a vastly more talented team are much more impressive than those who can get a team that is vastly more talented to play hard against a weaker opponent.

/ / / / / / /

Building a confident staff is essential to developing students who take risks. And our goal as educators is not to reflect society but to cultivate it. Understand the roles your school culture has and be mindful of the destabilization that will— and that will need to—occur when you mess with those roles. Remember that working to build an intentional culture includes a need to destabilize and allow for people within the culture to escape.

CHAPTER 9

Settling the Blame: It's Never Policies or Programs

We can get caught up in things
that do not matter and that
muddy the water.

The whole idea behind looking through the lens of organizational culture is to help people. With a focus on people, not programs, we are better able to make changes. Sometimes we may act as if programs have wills of their own, as if programs are able to make decisions and solve problems. When we talk about programs, we mean people, but by referring to the program we tend to let "people" off the hook. With nobody to take the blame (or credit), we are unable to take any steps. We have a built-in excuse as to why things don't work and why we have to try to manage around these hurdles rather than removing them.

Is there a program or a policy that your school struggles with or one that seems to be working well? Chances are that the responses will not be the same at every school. Some schools will be struggling with the ones you find valuable, and some will be enjoying success with the ones you are ready to trash. What is up with that? If you find yourself reaching for reasons that are unrelated to the people you have implementing these programs and policies, then read on as we explore some examples.

Professional Dress: A Policy

Although we, the authors of this book, disagree on some of the specific ideas in this section, we both agree in principle that one area that many educational leaders find to be a challenge is the professional dress of their faculty and staff. Society as a whole seems to be less formal than it was 30 years ago, when it would be hard to imagine wearing jeans to church or showing up to an interview wearing a ball cap. Our experiences have provided many stories about the way people dress for certain occasions, and some of these stories are about what teachers wear when they teach. One way to think about this is to ask yourself if professional dress is a "make or break." In other words, is it a cause-and-effect variable? If your worst performing teacher wore a tuxedo to work, would his classroom performance be dramatically improved? If your best performing teacher wore faded jeans, would she suddenly become ineffective? Obviously the answer to both questions is no, but that does not mean there is *no* relationship between dress and effectiveness. It is just not a one-to-one causal relationship.

Rather than center on the narrow area, or definition, of professional dress (remember from the last chapter that the school that underperformed defined student achievement only as test scores), maybe this discussion could fall under the umbrella of professionalism. Working to establish an environment of being professional in how we act, treat others, follow through, and dress may be a more healthy and reasonable approach. Too often we focus on narrow things that matter to us personally, but in the bigger picture of effectiveness, they are not the most essential components.

There are days and subject matter areas that may require a flexible dress code for teachers. Would you want your most innovative teacher to be held back from doing an activity or taking a field trip that would require a violation of the "faculty dress code"? Did your school once have a teacher who dressed very sloppily a few times, and now it operates under a school board policy that makes good teachers feel uncomfortable?

If professional dress is essential to you personally, there are things you can do to reinforce that idea on the days when staff are more likely to dress more formally, such as parent-teacher conferences, the first day of school, and Back to School Night. For example, you may comment directly to an individual ("I like that tie") or in a Friday Focus (Whitaker, Whitaker, & Lumpa, 2013) to the whole faculty. You could say something like this: "Several parents commented on what a wonderful group of teachers they met last night. They were so complimentary of the way we greeted them, how friendly we were, and even how we dressed!" The point is, if you want a school culture that embraces this type of professional decorum, then praise it.

Most school cultures expect teachers to dress a bit more formally when an event calls for interaction with the community. And we know that when we ask people to dress comfortably, they tend to relax more and may be happier. Yet there is no research proving that dress affects learning. Some head coaches wear sweats to the Super Bowl. Farmers do not need to wear ties when they teach their children how to raise cattle. However, if you have teachers struggling with classroom management, you might suggest they try dressing more professionally as a start.

However you as a school leader want your teachers to dress, the culture will have the last word. Regardless of the policy, the real interpretation will be deployed by veteran faculty each day. To change this part of the culture we would *not* suggest adopting a new rule. Instead, start with the new teachers. If this issue really matters to you, you could ask prospective candidates in interviews what they would wear on a typical day of school, how often they would wear a tie, what they think of teachers wearing jeans, and so on. Setting a tone and expectation in an interview makes it easier for you to reinforce your preference once the new teachers are employed. The culture will try to make them feel silly, so be prepared to have strong veteran teachers who agree with you available to support them.

Our goal in this section is not to provide a commentary on professional dress. It is an example of how we can get caught up in things that do not matter and that muddy the water when we attempt to bring about changes that really will make a difference. Professional dress is more about *appropriate* dress than it is about wearing a tie or sweats. This is one of the biggest issues some teachers and principals wrestle with, only because the culture does not align with the rules. Remember, the unwritten rules always win out over the written rules. Quit complaining about the sloppily dressed teachers and start praising the ones who dress as you prefer.

Clip Up, Clip Down:
A Classroom Management Strategy

There have always been and will always be a plethora of classroom management strategies. Assertive discipline, Class Dojo, red-yellow-green, students' names on the board, and multiple versions of each of these will regularly fade in and out of education. Heck, if they all work, then do all of them at the same time! But always remember, programs are never the problem and programs are never the solution. Any weak teacher can make a potentially good program look bad.

One popular approach to classroom management in many elementary classrooms is *clip up, clip down*. If a student misbehaves, the teacher moves a clip with the student's name down on a board, and if the student behaves appropriately, the clip is moved up. We find it interesting that some outstanding teachers use this approach, and so do some who are not so outstanding. If a teacher regularly engages students so that behavior-related disruptions are minimal and she resolves such occasional disruptions with a calm downward movement of the clip, we have great faith that the approach will work masterfully for that teacher.

Why do we mention this approach? Because it is an example of how something can be misinterpreted and misused. If a principal observes teachers successfully using *clip up, clip down*, he may think the reason the teachers are effective is because they use this approach. He may even mandate it for all the teachers in the school, or at least require it for all new faculty members.

If a teacher does not start the class in a professional and appropriate manner and then tries to use *clip down* as a threat, we have great faith the approach will not work. The teacher will be so busy moving clips there will not be much time to do anything else. Then the principal may find out about this issue (a weak teacher struggling with a new approach) and outlaw the use of *clip up, clip down*. The same thing happens with the next strategy, and the next, and so on.

Rather than individually addressing teachers who are struggling or ineffective, it is much easier to mandate or eliminate ideas, depending on how they are used by ineffective teachers. How often do principals, districts, or even entire states issue new rules or mandates because someone, somewhere, handled something unprofessionally or incorrectly? Have you ever had to complete an incredibly complicated form just to order a new stapler? The form is probably the result of someone, somewhere, at some time misusing funds—or even worse, someone hearing that someone, somewhere, at some time had misused funds. Thus we all suffer the consequences of ineffective leadership. Rather than deal with one person's transgression, a new process is put in place that everyone is now required to follow—and the person who caused it probably isn't going to follow it in any case!

In some schools, this is how things are done, and nobody thinks it is weird. The new teachers may look around in disbelief for a few moments, but they soon learn to be quiet and go with the flow. In some schools, every time someone breaks a rule, a new rule is established. Indiana recently passed a traffic law that prevents people from driving the speed limit in the fast lane if other drivers want to drive faster. In other words, the law made it illegal to prevent someone from breaking a traffic law. In some cultures, if you see someone doing something stupid, you are expected to let that person be stupid.

#CelebrateMonday: Busting a Culture

Some of the most gratifying feedback we have received on our earlier book, *School Culture Rewired*, has been from people who have used it as an impetus to initiate and lead change in their own setting and maybe even do something that has a worldwide impact. One such change has come to be called by its Twitter hashtag, #CelebrateMonday.

Typically, many people consider Monday to be a day when it is OK to be half asleep or to complain about being in a bad mood. It is not a single person who causes this to take place; it is the culture's expectation. There is no inherent reason we have to be in a bad mood on Monday and a good mood on Friday. Actually, if we allow ourselves to be miserable on

Monday, we are losing 20 percent of the week to our own frame of mind—quite a steep price to pay. And educators have to realize that many students come to school on Monday with anticipation because being in school is better than being in their home environment; for some of them, the weekend is the least enjoyable part of the week.

A reader of *School Culture Rewired*, Sean Gaillard, chose to do something about this situation, and the ripple effects have been astonishing. Sean is the principal of John F. Kennedy High School in Winston-Salem, North Carolina. After reading the book, he was intrigued by the possibility of "busting a culture" by "celebrating" Monday. He decided to try this not only for his own school but also to create something that could affect schools everywhere.

Sean told us more about his experience in an interview. He had read in *School Culture Rewired* how Monday gives us "permission" to be miserable. He felt that the assumption was not inherently true, but somehow we have allowed it to be so. He also felt that educators as a profession were not doing nearly enough to celebrate all of the wonderful things they do on a daily basis (including on Mondays!), and he wanted more opportunities to recognize and value educators. Around the same time, he had started using Twitter to market and promote his school. The first specific thing he did was to introduce the topic at a faculty meeting and ask, "How hard is it to celebrate Monday?" His faculty agreed that there is no cost to giving shout-outs to students and others who are also our personal heroes in education. Having just discovered Twitter "chats," he wanted to start a chat that celebrates the many positives in the education profession.

Sean started by letting others on Twitter know on Sundays what he was planning to do the next day to #CelebrateMonday in his school and his life. Incredibly, within a few weeks, his idea started trending on Twitter. It quickly became one of the top 10 topics week after week and across time zones worldwide. Rather than accepting the status quo by thinking that nothing could be done about people's attitudes about Monday, Sean actually has led a charge that has affected not only his school but also thousands of educators and students around the world. By observing and joining this movement, you can find and share dozens of ideas of how to #CelebrateMonday in your own school and life. Sean challenges all educators to share their reasons for celebrating the first day of the school week in a positive fashion.

Sean's idea has had an influence internationally and is trending on Twitter. He began his effort in his first year as a school principal, and his teachers were immediately taking pictures and showing off their students and the school. "Now, I and our teachers look forward to Mondays," he told us. "We are all excited about seeing what shout-outs everyone is going to give and receive."

One thing we always wonder about when we make changes is push-back. How will our effort be received by naysayers? Sean shared that he initially did hear from people with comments like "Oh, you're the Monday guy" or "Oh, you celebrate Twitter." Such reactions are perfect examples of cultural push-back. Some people *want* to be miserable on Monday. Some people want to be miserable *every* day. They are hoping other people will quit being happy and optimistic. Even fellow principals scoffed about #CelebrateMonday at meetings. Some people apparently want Mondays to remain miserable. It makes one wonder what they are protecting.

But the widespread enthusiasm for Sean's initiative outweighs the pushback. He receives notes thanking him for helping people fall back in love with education. In some notes, educators shared that they were going to leave the profession but that #CelebrateMonday gave them permission to remember all of the positive differences that teachers make every day. Sean feels it's not the hashtag that's important; it's the mindset and the people behind it. He has heard from people in Germany, England, and Argentina, to name just a few places (apparently the tendency to hate Mondays is an international phenomenon). Beyond the international, the movement has become extraterrestrial. While on the International Space Station, U.S. astronaut Jeff Williams (@Astro_Jeff) shared a picture of the Florida Keys and added the #CelebrateMonday hashtag.

When we asked Sean whether he was affecting the climate or the culture, he replied that he thought his effort was affecting both. He personally hasn't missed a Monday since he started #CelebrateMonday, and that consistency is an essential component of its success. As we know, if we change the climate and never revert, the change becomes imbedded as part of the culture. Sean feels every Monday is now like a holiday, and it is the day that people in his school most look forward to. As he told us, "I never want to miss that day."

We offer our own thanks to Sean, an amazing person and leader.

The Daily Difference

Although at first it may not be noticeable, the examples we have provided here of professional dress, *clip up, clip down*, and #CelebrateMonday share many similarities. One of them is the fact it really is up to one person to get a small group to start something. If one teacher dresses more professionally, some people will notice and possibly upgrade their own fashion—but maybe they won't. To make a difference, you have to keep doing what is right even if others do wrong. And just because one person does not notice and change something, it doesn't mean that no one does. Additionally, such things as insecurity or other reasons may cause the changes in people to be more subtle than you might hope. Rather than wearing a tie, perhaps they wear socks that match—or that do not have holes in them. Although this change is not visible to you, it is visible to them and their own self-worth. It becomes symbolic.

The challenge does not start by trying to get *everyone* to do something; it starts by getting *someone* to do something. We can never start by changing a whole culture. We start by changing something small—a routine, a story, or maybe just transforming a frown into a smile—and sticking with it every day so that eventually it becomes part of the culture.

/ / / / / / /

Think about this: No one ever used to wear a seat belt; now we feel uncomfortable without one. Smoking used to be cool; now the perception is remarkably different. Such changes do not start all at once. They occur one day, one person at a time. And that person keeps doing it until gradually we get to where we want to be. A casual jogger may never be a world-class marathon runner, but perhaps she can enjoy a guilt-free ice cream cone. Be the culture you want to see. Be it every day. See you on #CelebrateMonday!

CHAPTER 10

Solving Problems
with Professional
Learning
Communities

We tend to be social animals and are more effective in packs, so why not use this hard wiring to our advantage?

I n the previous chapter we discussed how the key to leading change is never policies or programs. Yet that contention can be confusing and difficult to deal with because new mandates and program ideas are constantly being implemented that can help facilitate changes in culture and in people. In this chapter we look at one popular idea, professional learning communities (PLCs), not from the lens of whether it is right or wrong (because programs are neither the problem nor the solution), but instead using it to understand what happens to and with culture and people when something new is implemented. Our exploration can also assist in understanding why some things work in certain schools and not others, as well as why they work with some teachers and not others—even in the same school.

What Are PLCs, Really?

Given the push for school leaders to become more aware of the concept of school culture, we find many strategies being implemented to make culture more useful. We tend to be social animals and are more effective in packs, so why not use this hard wiring to our advantage? And why not make smaller packs within the larger pack? In fact, this already happens without the help of leadership. All schools have cliques, and some cliques have the strength of a subculture. We think of departments, grade levels, teams, planning times, room location, and other elements as natural divisions, or subdivisions, of a school. These divisions may or may not be intentional efforts. One intentional strategy is to create a smaller group of teachers and call it a professional learning community, or PLC.

A PLC typically consists of three to eight teachers who share a cohort of students, a grade level, or a subject area. These groups meet on a regular basis to discuss a variety of topics relevant to student achievement. In an ideal setting, this collaboration provides a venue for teachers to share successes and challenges, trade ideas, and create new supports or structures for struggling students.

It is important to realize that PLCs differ considerably from one school to another in terms of their effectiveness. In general, they tend to reflect the traits of the larger school culture. The most successful ones often develop in schools with an overall collaborative culture. Conversely, they may be relatively ineffective in schools that lack such a culture. Sometimes, however, a PLC develops into a subculture that becomes strong enough to influence the decisions of the school administrators.

The Smartest Person in the Room

Earlier in this book we noted a trendy saying in education: "The smartest person in the room is the room." This implies that collectively the group is smarter than the individuals in it, and the end result will be the best possible decision. In a perfect world—or a perfectly collaborative situation—this may be true, but unfortunately this is not the real world. Often the dominant or the most vocal personality ends up swaying the group in making a decision. A better saying might be "The smartest person in the room should be the room."

We have all been in situations where the decision made was not the wisest one. The dynamic of that group or subculture may or may not have caused that to happen. We have to remember that, in general, effective teachers like to meet with effective teachers and ineffective teachers like to meet with ineffective teachers. When we mix the two groups, we are playing dice, not chess. But our goal should always be to ensure that the final result is what is best for the students.

One PLC may continually brainstorm ways to succeed as much as possible with individual students or discuss the most effective way to ensure student learning of a difficult concept. The members may openly share ideas that work for them or struggles they face in teaching a particular individual. This is the type of setting that can make a PLC powerful. It allows the knowledge of one to become the knowledge of all. However, as we suggested earlier, not all PLCs are created equal.

Another professional learning community in the same school could turn into what seems like a regular gripe fest. Its meetings may routinely consist of little more than a roundtable sharing of complaints toward administrators. One teacher who is not known for being a positive person may continually complain about her most challenging student—we'll call him Kenny. In the best-case scenario, the skills and abilities represented by the PLC as a whole *could* use a session to brainstorm solutions, challenging the teacher who raised the issue. Perhaps once this negative teacher heard a solution, she might give Kenny a fresh start. The problem would be closer to being solved, and this teacher might now enter the next PLC meeting with a positive and optimistic tone. Notice that we said "could."

Unfortunately, another possible outcome to this scenario may have that teacher continually making excuses for why the ideas will not work and actually dampening the tone for the group as a whole. Not only do others begin to complain about Kenny, they start to create a gripe session about their own "Kennys." The PLC actually becomes a source of frustration for the more positive members and a counterproductive experience in terms of the "professional learning" of the school community.

This discussion is not an attempt to disparage PLCs—not at all. Our purpose is to share our concerns with school leaders who may simply create PLCs and then assume a problem has been solved, when all they actually did was go to the hardware store and buy a new tool. If the existing culture has never had PLCs, then it may not like having PLCs. The feeling may be that teachers have gotten along fine without them in the past.

Is it possible for the PLC to improve teachers and for teachers to improve the PLC?

Would you like to know if your PLCs are actually a positive part of the culture and are making a difference? Simply ask teachers not to meet one week. Make up a reason—testing, holidays, whatever. Then see who cares, who is happy, who is complaining, and who is secretly meeting anyway. If PLCs are part of your school culture, you will have a substantial number of people who are confused and may go ahead and meet anyway. Now do a deeper test. If there are groups that are still meeting, are they beneficial or counterproductive? Have the PLCs become a lifeline of support, or have they become the main venue for increasing the negative energy through venting and complaining?

Professional learning communities are *potentially* a valuable tool that has been used productively in many school settings. In others, their value can vary widely from group to group. Some groups see the PLC as the most valuable resource in their school, but others, not so much. Some schools reap few benefits from these meetings. But as we have noted, PLCs are neither the problem nor the solution. They are designed to be a tool that can be a tremendous asset for collaboration only if the culture is designed to support and allow valuable open sharing among teachers. A leader needs to make a conscious decision to educate faculty on how to best use this community time. The leader must also be aware of the pulse of each group and provide training and support as needed for teachers to take full advantage of what PLCs can do. By starting with one or two groups that might most benefit from a PLC collaborative model, a school may develop a ritual of sharing that could then be used as training grounds for others within the same setting. In other words, one meeting per month could be dedicated to two groups meeting together.

Looking for and working with points of least resistance can greatly facilitate the initial implementation of a concept such as PLCs. When a PLC is established and can demonstrate its actual value, the concept can spread more easily among others in the same school. If the PLC model is forced upon everyone, some groups may actually work against the concept.

The point is, we need to make sure that PLC stands for "professional learning community" and not "pretty lousy concept" or "personal lounging club." These structures can be great for collaboration in any school as long as the culture allows it and the leader is intentional about their successful implementation.

What Matters Most: Leadership and Culture

Although this chapter is about professional learning communities, we have used this concept as an example to demonstrate how all things depend on leadership and culture. Just as assertive discipline and project-based learning can be a success or a failure in two adjacent classrooms, the same is true of almost any program or idea. The success or failure of those programs and ideas is often more an indicator of where a school culture is than it is an indicator of their inherent value.

In the classroom of a great teacher, pretty much any "discipline plan" would work well because the teacher is effective in general and the "plan" is an integral part of the day. If the same approach doesn't work in the classroom of a less effective teacher, it is usually because the underlying structures are not there; nothing would work to manage the students because the teacher has trouble managing herself.

Remember, anytime we try to make a change we challenge the culture of an organization. The outcome can be a positive or a negative, but it almost always is an indication of where we are in terms of culture. It reminds us of the old saying: "Change is inevitable; growth is optional." School improvement is a never-ending journey, but one that we are all glad to be taking.

Here is an activity you might bring to your next PLC meeting. Ask the following questions of the group and hypothesize about (1) what might happen during the meeting and (2) what the PLC might take away from the experience:

- Ask an honor student to attend a meeting and ask him or her what is working and what is not working in the school.

- Ask a student who most teachers struggle with to attend a meeting and ask him or her what is working and what is not working in the school.

- Ask a parent, a cook, a bus driver, or the superintendent to attend a meeting; does anyone act differently during the meeting?

- Ask the PLC members to list the three biggest issues at the school and compare the lists to see if everyone is at the same school.

- Ask the PLC members to list the three most effective teachers in the building.

- Invite a new teacher who is considering working at your school to attend a meeting and let that person do most of the talking.

- Have each participant tell a story of their greatest accomplishment as a teacher, in their careers, for this year, for this week.

- Go outside and walk around the grounds as you meet.

- Do a book study, starting with this book, this chapter.

- Discuss the most embarrassing thing that ever happened to you in class that other staff never found out about.

If we want PLCs to have the effect they are designed to have, then we should be able to do most of these activities and walk away stronger. If anyone does not come out of a PLC meeting feeling better or stronger, then we may want to ask, why do we have PLCs?

///////

In the next chapter we turn to a question that has been researched for years: whether it is possible to quantify decision making. Don't get your hopes up. We do not claim to have cracked that code, but there may be a way to understand culture and change dynamics using numbers as a basis for clarity.

CHAPTER 11

Leading by
the Numbers

The magnitude, timing, and proximity of events will determine the effect on culture.

The concept of culture can seem very esoteric and understanding it can be challenging. However, looking at it in a quantitative way may help facilitate an understanding of the opportunities it offers and provide a new way to describe the process of organizational change. As we think about helping people and improving the ability of culture to solve problems, this chapter introduces a new way to envision leadership.

Leadership is a construct that has enjoyed decades, if not centuries, of philosophical debate. Many theories exist to help us understand how leadership affects human behavior. "Leadership by the numbers" (LBN) is an attempt to help people understand leadership through the use of mathematics. No doubt that statement makes some of you ready to quit reading about now. We ask that you give us one more paragraph.

Before we had the Richter scale, if we wanted to describe how destructive an earthquake was, we could only tell each other stories. Now, when we say "7.2," we have an idea as to what happened. Similarly, tornados are measured on the Fujita scale, and hurricanes have categories. Numbers never give us the whole story, but they provide a degree of reliability when we make comparisons. LBN provides us with a new language to discuss, compare, and contrast events and how they might influence leadership behaviors, as well as inform us when something in the culture is changing. To further explain this unique leadership approach, we shall use it to better understand the concept of organizational culture.

LBN: Changing a Culture

Organizational cultures come in various strengths. The degree to which the group demonstrates cohesiveness, loyalty, and commitment will determine that level of strength. A strong culture has high levels of cohesiveness. A weak culture will not have much loyalty within. Strong cultures are more difficult to change. For purposes of this theory (LBN), cultural strength is located on a scale from 1 to 10, with 10 being the strongest. There is no zero because there is never "no" level of culture.

To change a culture, or a significant part of a culture, an event (E) needs to occur. Cultures are changed by events, not attitudes. Attitudes (which include such things as satisfaction, efficacy, and morale) are by-products of how an event was addressed by the culture and thus cannot serve as vehicles for change; experiences change cultures. The magnitude, timing, and proximity of events will determine the effect on culture. An event with a large magnitude will change a culture more easily than a weaker event. The magnitude of events could be located on a scale of 1 to 20, with 20 being strongest. No event can create "no" culture or cause culture to completely disappear.

Hang on. This explanation is about to get messy if you are not in a quiet place. The following hypotheses explain how cultures change:

- Cultures and associated activities tend to persist.

- If the magnitude of a new event is weak, the culture persists.

- If the magnitude of a new event persists, the culture changes.

Both the current culture (Ca) and the next culture (Cb) will exist within a scale of 1 to 10 indicating cultural strength, with 10 being the strongest (see Figure 11.1). Ca10 is 20 points away from Cb10. Ca1 is 1 point away from Cb1. In the figure, two cultures (each one represented by a bracket) are juxtaposed in terms of levels of strength.

Changing a culture requires introducing an event (E[1–20]) that has sufficient magnitude and proximity (local connection) so as to move from the Ca part of the scale to the Cb part. All events will test the culture. Some strengthen it, and some weaken it—developments that are necessary for it to move toward another culture. Moving from Ca1 to Cb1 will not require much of an event (magnitude 1). However, moving from Ca5 to Cb5 will require a significant event (magnitude 10) or a series of less significant events with a total magnitude of 10, that occur within a compressed time frame. Thus it is not only the magnitude of the event that can change a culture, but also the time frame in which this event (or several events) occurs. Many events within a shorter time frame will change a culture more easily than these same events occurring with weeks or months between them. Several smaller events can have the strength of a major event if they persist or occur within a shorter time frame.

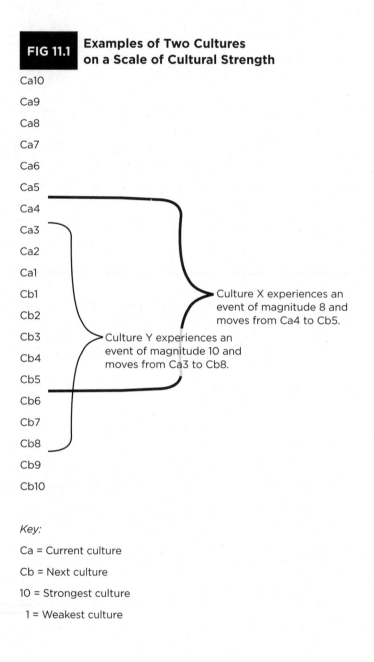

FIG 11.1   **Examples of Two Cultures on a Scale of Cultural Strength**

Ca10

Ca9

Ca8

Ca7

Ca6

Ca5

Ca4

Ca3

Ca2

Ca1

Cb1

Cb2

Cb3

Cb4

Cb5

Cb6

Cb7

Cb8

Cb9

Cb10

Culture X experiences an event of magnitude 8 and moves from Ca4 to Cb5.

Culture Y experiences an event of magnitude 10 and moves from Ca3 to Cb8.

Key:

Ca = Current culture

Cb = Next culture

10 = Strongest culture

1 = Weakest culture

A shorter time frame suggests that events have shelf lives. The impact of events will decay when too much time elapses between them. Changes need time compression (T) and proximity (P) to reach critical mass. To experience a new activity at low frequency and low magnitude, in a faraway place, will not change the local culture.

The idea of needing proximity suggests that some events may happen in other regions that may or may not affect the local community. Proximity is something that prompts an emotional response to such a degree that people will question their current system as an effective mechanism for survival. If a tornado destroys a local school, then the community is very much affected. If a tornado destroys a school 500 miles away, then the local community may not sense that same level of affect. Thus the proximity of the event provides a degree of local connection.

To change a culture, we need to understand the relevant variables: (1) the strength of the current culture (Ca), (2) the time frame (T) given, (3) what events (E) are possible that will have proximity (P), and (4) how strong the next culture (Cb) will need to be to adopt the changes and become resistant (stronger) to the next change. Let's look more closely at some of these variables.

As we have explained, cultural strength is measured on a scale from 1 to 10. In terms of specific traits, a strength of 1 would describe a culture that is very fragmented, with isolated members having some association. In a school, this would be a group of adults who happen to work in the same building. At the other end of the scale, a strength of 10 would suggest a cult, with individuals forsaking any personal identity and surrendering all assets and resources to the good of the group. In a school, the feeling of being a family may rank as an 8.

Events, as we have noted, can be measured on a scale of 1 through 20, as well as proximity. On the scale, an event such as rolling one's eyes is a 1, and the end of the world is a 20. It is also important to note that events can be man-made or occur naturally. How and why certain events in history have or have not affected the culture of a country or region can be debated. What singular events changed the way we go about our lives? Which movements seemed to take forever to get off the ground? What has died on the vine? Consider these examples:

- Civil rights
- Terrorism
- Sputnik
- 9/11
- Rock and roll music
- Cognitive coaching

As a leader, note that you can take advantage of events to improve your culture. The *change effect* is a phenomenon that occurs when change is experienced by a group. During this time of uncertainty, other changes will be perceived as less intrusive. The shock value of the initial first strike (change) will camouflage additional minor changes. Thus the best time to bring small changes to the group is when a bigger change has occurred. As people gasp for breath and enter a state of recovery, they are unprepared for, and perhaps indifferent to, other minor changes that may be happening around them.

A Language for Understanding Culture

In schools, we never want to change the whole culture. Instead, we become aware of parts of a culture that are no longer useful. Often a change in the school's culture is simply how the group solves problems; cultures provide a framework for solving problems. Thus, as we have said before, culture is not a problem to be solved (neither are the concepts of engagement, teaching, inclusion, or diversity; these are devices we use to solve problems). Culture is a tool we use to survive. Much like a computer, culture is human technology. PLCs are tools to make collaboration easier. PLCs are not collaborative cultures, nor are they guarantees that a collaborative culture will exist.

LBN provides leaders with a language for examining culture and responding to cultural norms with more precision than relying on feelings or instincts. Figure 11.2 helps to clarify this idea. (Schools that exhibit levels of strength beyond an 8, as well as events that exist beyond a 10, are very rare and thus not useful when thinking about LBN; however, we need to show the whole scale for perspective.) Here's the payoff for reading this chapter. For purposes of changing a school culture, the shaded areas in the figure are most relevant to school leaders. To create the conditions necessary for a cultural change, the appropriate event(s) will need to occur within a particular time frame. To reach beyond this shaded area could create a level of disequilibrium that would be difficult to manage—too much uncertainty and stress can allow any fool to step up and claim to be the leader. Any singular event beyond the scope of E10 could destabilize the group to a point beyond maintaining the integrity of the current system. Figure 11.2 presents the range of possibilities.

Here are some additional thoughts to consider:

- Is Ca5 closer to Cb5 (a quantum wormhole or shortcut) than the linear distance? We would rather work with people who care about the wrong things than people who care about nothing. Ca5 could be a culture caring about the wrong things.

FIG 11.2	Range of Possibilities for Strength of Culture and Event Magnitude											
Ca10												
Ca9												
Ca8												
Ca7												
Ca6												
Ca5												
Ca4												
Ca3												
Ca2												
Ca1												
Cb1												
Cb2												
Cb3												
Cb4												
Cb5												
Cb6												
Cb7												
Cb8												
Cb9												
Cb10												
	E1	E2	E3	E4	E5	E6	E7	E8	E9	E10	E11	E12

Key: Ca = Existing culture Cb = New culture E = Event 1 = Weakest
10 = Strongest

- Do you have a comfortable level of devotion to a culture, whether it be a negative or a positive place? Generally speaking, that level is home court.

- Is it possible that some people do not know how to live in a weak or a strong culture?

Applying LBN to Other Aspects of Leadership

We realize the last few pages were full of language that may have seemed irrelevant to what you need to do tomorrow. But LBN is simply a new way to look at leadership. We tried to put a number on everything and then see how those numbers compare: that is, does the force of an event change the leadership style and thus cause the culture to react and possibly begin to change? We will try to make all this stuff useful, but we need to go abstract again for just a minute or two.

Each of us has an attitude about the different things in life we face (for example, a flat tire on the highway, a thunderstorm at night, long lines in the grocery store, Monday mornings). Our attitudes are usually made obvious through our behaviors (for example, laughing, crying, rolling our eyes, cursing). Although our personalities can limit the range of attitudes we may express, there are other variables that influence our attitudes. Your attitude and associated behaviors are choices you make to feel a certain way, and you learned them earlier in life. Chances are if you lose your temper when you experience a flat tire, it is because someone you respected earlier in life did the same thing.

Imagine any one of life's themes—work, home life, hobby, religion, traffic—and where you might fall on a scale that ranges from the most positive attitude (A 10) to the most negative (A $^-$10) when you are in these environments. Is your attitude different when you are in traffic as opposed to playing golf or fishing? Or compare your attitude at church and at work.

What is your typical range in each of these situations? Is it possible that a ceiling exists for each one, meaning that you have a limited capacity to improve, yet an unlimited capacity to decline? Is there a number for each situation that you have become accustomed to, thus improving or declining may cause a sense of discomfort? How much of this is determined by those you choose to be friends with, work with, read about, or watch from a distance (virtually or in the real world)? Can you be an A 7 and live around A 2s?

Does Figure 11.3, which shows range of attitudes, resemble Figure 11.1? Well, that is not a coincidence. Wherever or whoever you are now could be measured and compared with whomever you could be in the future, just like your school's culture—at least the LBN theory believes it to be possible. The range by which a person can display a positive attitude is limited; however, the negative attitude does not have a limit. Range is determined by personality and environment. Leaping from the negative to the positive range—from A ⁻6 to A 5, as shown in the figure—does not occur easily. And we believe that without strong leadership, slipping into the negative range is easier. Doing nothing rarely causes people to get better.

A Recap

Leadership by the numbers is a way for leaders to reflect on their leadership behaviors and decisions using mathematics. Calling an approaching weather event a Category 5 hurricane ensures that people will respond more appropriately than

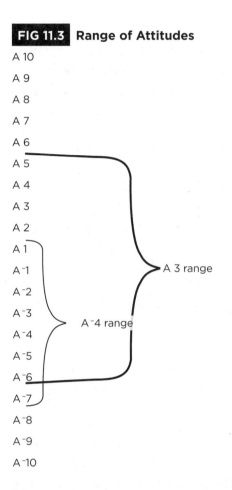

FIG 11.3 **Range of Attitudes**

telling them a big storm is coming. With these scales, the necessary events can be identified, thus preventing issues of doing
too little or too much, or doing it too late. Your capacity as a
leader, the strength of your organization, and the magnitude
of events that your organization experiences can be placed on
a scale. The information from this scale will provide a unique
lens for viewing your work. Once you understand LBN, stating
that your school needs to move from a 2.5 to a 3.7 has more
meaning than stating the school needs to improve.

Applying this same concept to the interactions between people and culture can also be beneficial. In Chapter 1 we talked about the relationship between teacher climate and student climate, how the up-and-down movement of either one causes the other to adjust in some way.

This same thing applies between culture and people. If we think of culture and people in a quantitative way, as we add additional talented staff members and simultaneously improve the capabilities of existing staff, this inherently improves the quality of the culture. If we improve the culture, this inherently improves the capabilities of the staff members. The sum of the people in an organization equals the culture, and the culture affects the ability of an organization to help its members grow. It also determines the type of talent that wants to join the group. High-functioning, positive groups attract people who are high-functioning and positive, and as we add people with those traits, it is much more likely that the culture will follow. And the opposite is also true. Negative people are comfortable around other negative people. That is why it is essential that leaders cultivate their cultures while they simultaneously nurture, grow, and attract talent to help move the culture in a positive direction.

Can leaders reduce everything to numbers and simply do math problems as their schools face various events? That is not for us to determine. Rather, LBN is simply a new way to look at leadership and possibly extend our thinking beyond what we have been taught.

If we confused you with this chapter, we apologize. If we have intrigued you and challenged your thinking on leadership, there will be more to come. Another way to frame this thinking is to look backward. Were there significant events at your school or in the world at large that caused people or the culture to change? Were there events that happened that could have had this effect but the leadership did not take advantage of them? Have there been years when a large number of new faculty and staff were added? Did you make sure that these new people were protected and allowed to form their own subculture from which the school significantly improved, or were the new staff members divided and thrown into individual departments and grade levels, thus minimizing the opportunity for growth and change?

The concepts in this chapter are not intended to say that everything is inherently a clinical analysis and that the best person to lead a school is a quantum physics professor. Instead, it is intended to provide another lens through which to look at opportunities as they arise and make sure they are used in a way that provides the most benefit to the organization and support for cultural growth. Without being aware of these possibilities, we may see major occurrences as things we must survive and wait for them to pass—like going into the storm cellar and hoping nothing changes. But with the proper understanding, these events can actually be opportunities—and even excuses—to instigate quick and major movement in the culture.

///////

In the next chapter we revisit a concept we introduced earlier—the difference between climate and culture. More specifically, we examine how the gap between the two can actually be a useful space and how climate can serve as a leverage point in the effort to change culture.

CHAPTER 12

Developing New
Organizational
Habits

The interval between resistance of a new idea and its acceptance occurs when someone goes above and beyond the traditional norm.

arlier we emphasized that organizational culture and organizational climate are not the same thing. In *School Culture Rewired* (Gruenert & Whitaker, 2015) we devoted an entire chapter to making that point. Our intent here is not to continue that argument but rather to assume that you agree and to explain what that means for school leaders. One idea worth investigating is that if culture and climate are not the same thing, then how are they connected? If they are not the same thing, what about the space between them—the gap? Is there something in this gap that might be useful to know about? When does a change in the climate (drift) become something that changes the culture?

Attitude, Personality, and Disposition

We have used "attitude" as an analogy for climate, and "personality" as an analogy for culture. When thinking about people, the space between attitude and personality could be identified as one's disposition. Our disposition is what we tend to do in given situations. For schools, the construct of disposition might be identified as the rituals we practice—our organizational tendencies or habits. We use various elements of culture to identify the type of culture we have, and we use these elements as leverage points to shape a new culture. Thus changing a culture may start with a change in the climate, which can be accomplished by changing a routine or a ritual.

Confusing? Stay with us, because this is important to under-stand. Climate may be *the* leverage point of culture.

Again, culture is made up of our values and beliefs; climate is how we currently feel. We usually do not choose how we feel (Brown, 2015); it is something we learn as we try to fit in. Our disposition is how we tend to feel given a certain situation. Consider the following metaphor. A restaurant menu offers a selection of items that fits the theme of that eatery; we will call that the restaurant's personality. From that menu (its person-ality) we will have a limited set of choices. We cannot order a hotdog at the local steakhouse, nor can we get a taco at the local Italian eatery. What we actually order that day we will call the climate. It is what is happening right now, in the pres-ent. It is what we choose, given the limited set of choices from the menu. Here is where it becomes fun. Our friends will know what we tend to order—our disposition. If we try to exper-iment with a new food, we can expect a response from our friends that may cause us to retract our new idea. "You have never ordered that in the past," they may say.

Think about what happens when you first attempt to change. If you work with traditionally grumpy people, they may be startled when you smile. A quick response—an attack—could be expressed as "What are you so happy about?" They are hoping you are just going through a temporary phase. Their grumpiness is trying to lower you back to what they think is normal. The people who consistently take an approach that goes against the culture can even be labeled as outsiders. Dis-gruntled comments like "They are always happy" or "There goes goodie-two-shoes" can brand someone as a person who doesn't belong.

The desire to fit in is one reason people associate with others who are like themselves. If you are always negative, then you feel normal (and validated) with like-minded colleagues, and it is now the positive people who don't fit in. What this means in terms of change is that some people may need to change peer groups as they try to change their attitude. Remember, climate is how we feel; culture tells us how we are *supposed* to feel. To remain in a culture that is changing, you must change the way you feel to align with the expectations of the culture, or you may leave the culture. In a school setting, you will either leave the school, or stay in the school and build your own clique.

This situation happens many times in our lives. For example, we could go through elementary and middle school with the same set of friends, but if some of them choose to begin drinking or using drugs, their actions can divide the group into cliques. This may even result in our referring to our former friends as "prudes" or "druggies," depending on which side of the divide we choose. Sports teams, cheerleading, and other extracurricular activities can also cause sorting and sifting. After we leave high school we may think such dividing is over, but unfortunately it is part of life's path. We may be more capable of dealing with it, but it is still something we face in personal and professional settings.

Schools operate under the same unwritten rules. Each school has a personality—a menu of predetermined responses. Each school has a disposition—a set of tendencies we can expect from it as it responds to certain situations. Each school has a climate—the response it chooses (orders from the menu) that day.

So what? If there is a space between culture and climate, and this space is equal to the concept of dispositions, what does it mean to those of us hoping to create a new school culture?

Using Rituals and Routines as Leverage Points

Dispositions are a set of habits. Organizational habits are rituals and routines. In Figure 12.1, we present a chart that outlines the differences between climate and culture. And, in the following list, we give ideas about rituals and routines that might represent leverage points that you can use to help positively affect the climate and culture in your school.

- Adding donuts to a meeting to help make attendees feel appreciated
- Greeting others with a smile can be contagious
- Making decisions as a group, not announcing predictable top-down demands
- Announcing special faculty/staff parking for employee(s) of the month
- Assigning random seats at faculty meetings to invite potential for new friends
- Making a point to focus on, post, and celebrate student work throughout the building
- Adjusting the local "speed limit" relative to how we work
- Celebrating testing as a chance to show what is learned, instead of as a distraction from teaching and learning
- Building risk taking into daily school life
- Being positive role models, because what others see us do is what they think we value most

FIG 12.1	Some Differences Between Climate and Culture

Culture . . .	Climate . . .
. . . is the group's personality.	. . . is the group's attitude.
. . . gives Mondays permission to be miserable.	. . . differs from Monday to Friday, February to May.
. . . provides for a limited way of thinking.	. . . creates a state of mind.
. . . takes years to evolve.	. . . is flexible, easy to change.
. . . is based on values and beliefs.	. . . is based on perceptions.
. . . can't be felt, even by group members.	. . . can be felt when you enter a room.
. . . is part of us.	. . . surrounds us.
. . . is "the way we do things around here."	. . . is "the way we feel around here."
. . . has allies and enemies.	. . . is a group's response to a situation.
. . . determines whether or not improvement is possible.	. . . is the first thing that improves when positive change is made.
. . . is in your head.	. . . is in your head.

Source: Adapted from *School Culture Rewired: How to Define, Assess, and Transform It* (p. 10), by S. Gruenert and T. Whitaker, Alexandria, VA: ASCD. Copyright © 2015 by ASCD. Adapted with permission.

Remember that the point at which something moves from being a temporary change (climate) to a more permanent status (culture) is seldom obvious to those who are doing it. But if we do make a temporary change, such as being friendly or celebrating Monday, and we never revert to the earlier behavior, the new behavior does become part of the culture. We are simply not sure of the start date. So, with that in mind, what does the time between temporary and permanent look like? How do we know when a new ritual or routine is beginning to stick (Heath & Heath, 2007)?

Navigating the Interval Between Resistance and Acceptance

The interval between resistance to a new idea and its acceptance occurs when someone goes above and beyond the traditional norm. If a new teacher independently decides to make positive phone calls to parents, this could be perceived as showing off or as a threat to the existing culture. Other teachers may tell the newbie that "we don't do that here" or "parents do not like to be bothered." It isn't inconceivable that the principal would hear from parents, who may comment that they have a message to call the teacher and wonder what is wrong. If the principal doesn't know what the call is about, the parents may wonder even more about what's going on at school.

Though this may seem silly, every organization has certain individuals who have set the level of effort regarding what is acceptable and normal. If these levels are exceeded, peer pressure may be exerted to return to the regular effort level.

Ironically, some parents can be involved in the effort for teachers to resume the normal effort level and to eliminate the positive initiative. For example, a parent may be upset if the teacher calls the "other" parent, especially if they are separated. Or, a busy parent may respond that he only wants to hear about emergencies. In addition, other teachers may resent the positive responses the teacher receives when she contacts parents with good news; any or all teachers could hear complaints from parents or students who have not received these plaudits and are resentful.

As you can imagine, these issues put a great deal of pressure to return to the culture of only calling parents with bad news.

However, if the teacher persists and other staff members and the principal join the fun, it can become a part of the new normal and infiltrate the culture. Just like the example of celebrating Monday, the tipping point can be one individual who wants to take a different path and is willing to continue in that direction, despite the discomfort of others inside and outside the organization.

Though the initial positive phone calls may only affect climate, it can become a part of the culture of the school if the school staff continues valuing and reinforcing student effort and accomplishment. The point is that what occurs in this gap between resistance and adoption determines whether the change was a temporary alteration or a permanent shift in the belief system.

Taking Advantage of the Gap

In this chapter we have asked you to think about the gap between climate and culture. There are organizational habits that ensure you keep doing what you are doing. Once in a while, someone may try to introduce a new habit, such as a new way to take attendance, a new way to do graduation, a new textbook, a new whatever. Most new things die off in the gap we have discussed here. But sometimes, something new sticks. Think about new ideas at your school that stuck and the ones that didn't. Looking at your list of your school's new habits, what kind of activities did you introduce that made them stick? Now create a list of new habits you would want your school to adopt. What activities might help them thrive? What could you start tomorrow to begin to change the culture without threatening it?

As a leader, you must also be aware of people who are altering their rituals and routines and provide encouragement and safety for those who are doing so in a positive way. Without this affirmation, they can receive too little support and no positive validation. Thus they may quickly revert back to the norm, and it may require twice the effort in the future for them to take a chance on changing themselves and eventually affecting the entire organization.

/ / / / / / /

For some people, successfully navigating the gap between climate and culture can be one indicator of successful leadership. Others may consider it a sign of good management. But what is the difference between leadership and management—and how does culture fit into the discussion? That is the topic of the next chapter.

CHAPTER 13

Allowing Culture to Manage

Cultures are designed to detect viruses, which typically come labeled as change—any change.

There has long been a debate about the difference between a leader and a manager. Although these two roles are interconnected, they do have a different purpose. What role might the culture play in this interaction?

If the culture is leading the school, then the principal is simply managing it. If the leader lets the culture manage the school, then the leader can lead the school. Semantics? Here is what we mean. In business we see a hierarchy that separates leaders and managers. Leaders tend to make more money and have a nicer office. It almost feels as though some people are more important than others. In education, management and leadership are both necessary; they should complement each other.

We believe leaders and managers serve two separate functions but are both working on the same team. Management involves oversight of daily operations, which usually includes the behaviors of people. If leaders are spending time chasing down the misbehaviors of other adults, then they may not have much time or energy left to invest in leadership.

Cultures can manage the behaviors of people. And they do this quite well. As you look at the following list, think about which ones are a function of peer pressure (culture) and which ones are directed by the leadership:

- Correcting student behavior
- Teachers' use of planning time
- Making a phone call to a parent
- Grading an essay
- Yelling at students
- Trusting students
- Showing up for work early or late; leaving work early or late
- Meeting deadlines

If leaders are spending too much time messing around with the peer-pressure functions, then they are not using their leadership to its fullest capacity, and they may be compromising their leadership capital when they do use it. Many principals were once assistant principals or deans, and their earlier administrative experiences focused on student discipline. They may have become very good at it, and now they seek to resolve those issues instead of "doing" leadership.

If a school has established a tone that expects teachers to treat students appropriately and teachers consistently behave professionally, then there is a much greater opportunity to lead significant change in the setting. But if a school faces continual classroom-management issues, with fires to be extinguished, then leadership can quickly be reduced to being reactionary.

Another thing to keep in mind is that many people who are placed in leadership roles are actually more comfortable with managing. As we stated, if an assistant principal has only dealt with discipline and supervision during her administrative career, potentially she feels much more comfortable in that area than she would with, perhaps, curriculum. So although we may want an administrator to be a leader, she may actually prefer or even insist on defining the principalship as a management role. However, once the educational leader is able to establish expectations, hire effectively, and teach faculty and staff best operational practices, there is now a window through which to pull others.

If the norm in a school's classrooms is escalating student misbehavior, then a great deal of administrative reacting will be required. If we do not teach bus drivers appropriate student-management skills, then we will always face transportation discipline issues. If we do not make teachers feel valued on a regular basis, then we may have an overabundance of lower-skilled substitute teachers to corral. These are important issues. Often we simply think the culture can handle them, that these are aspects of the school that do not have to be monitored before a school leader actually begins to lead. The prevalent feeling is to let the culture of the school manage the behaviors of students on buses (by the way, it is already doing so).

For example, think about teachers. If teachers are effective classroom managers, they may still not be where they need to be instructionally, but if they are not effective classroom managers, they will *never* be where they need to be instructionally. Working toward a culture that embraces appropriate practices by faculty and staff is an essential part of eventually leading the school toward the desired outcome. A collaborative and open culture is needed for the leader to lead. We cannot wait until every single person is on board with management practices before we shift into leadership mode, but we definitely need to get routines established to ensure that most people are doing things correctly.

Culture Builders

In the previous chapter we discussed how elements of climate, such as routines and rituals, can be used as leverage points for changing school culture. Leverage points are times when the culture is vulnerable to change. Some are natural occurrences, such as the beginning of school or during a change of leadership. Others are manufactured occurrences—the times when leaders can nudge the movement of a culture toward change without having to wait for the natural leverage times to arrive. We call these *culture busters*. They weaken the system to make it more open to change.

Now we want to talk about building the new culture and to discuss *culture builders*. When the organization responds to issues in a predictable and effective manner, the culture wins and gets stronger. We believe there are strategies leaders can use to nudge the culture toward becoming stronger as it improves. Cultures change when they are destabilized, or unfrozen (Lewin, 1936). During these times they are vulnerable to change—good or bad. Positive and negative leaders do their best work when the culture is experiencing disequilibrium. The point here is not just to bust up the culture and see what happens; school leaders need to have the next few steps planned out before any anticipated discomfort has a chance to take hold.

Here are some examples of culture builders:

- Giving praise in public and private
- Refining ceremonies
- Connecting to the past/alumni visits
- Validating people and rituals

- Applauding the effort, not just the results
- Celebrating small wins
- Identifying a new enemy (if the current "enemy" is the students or parents)
- Offering empathy
- Showing interest
- Offering forgiveness before risk taking
- Building new stories

Although none of these may be a shocking idea, what may surprise you is how much weight each one can carry. Using culture as a lens by which to think about these ideas leads us to consider *who* uses them and *when* they are used, as variables in this equation, just as much as *what* is said. Is it possible that a pat on the back from a good friend carries as much inspirational weight as an award given at a faculty meeting? Could the testimony of a former student provide more motivation than the governor proclaiming that yours is a Blue Ribbon school? Do people respond to empathy more than sympathy? If they know you care, you may have "permission" to make more mistakes.

Let's take a closer look at some of these culture builders to help you apply them (though not all at once) in your school. Think of them as steroids. They cannot be the only thing you do to make your school culture stronger, but they will certainly amplify your efforts.

Giving praise

Praise is an incredibly powerful tool if done correctly. There are few things more powerful than a well-placed compliment.

Going into a teacher's classroom and leaving her a note along the lines of "I was sitting in my office and I forgot what school was. I wanted to visit your classroom so I could remember. Thanks for being here for the students. Thanks for being here for me." This kind of message makes that teacher feel better, and can increase her resistance to the influence of peers who may not want her to try as hard or care as much.

This same approach can work on a schoolwide basis. If you would like teachers to be at their doors greeting students at the start of class, you can thank people individually who are out there sharing their warmth. You could also write in a staff memo or an e-mail message, "Today when I walked around I saw so many teachers at their doors smiling and welcoming students. It sure makes a difference. Thanks for taking the time to make students feel valued." No teacher is singled out in this message, but it is a positive reminder of what it is you want the school climate to be. And because this affects people's attitudes, it sets a tone or expectation that "If everybody else is doing it, I need to do it also." This is a powerful way for culture to help move individuals forward. This is letting the culture manage the attitudes of the faculty and staff—culture giving permission to climate to be friendly. In addition, what is being valued is something everyone can do. Rather than recognizing a talent that only a few possess, this is acknowledging something that everyone can do. It enables each person to feel and be a part of an evoiving culture.

Celebrating small wins

Do not wait until someone loses 20 pounds to compliment him on his diet. It is essential that you make people feel important regularly. Given the teacher shortages in so many locations, you need to make sure that you are doing everything you can to keep your strongest employees happy and satisfied. As we know, people are much more likely to quit their bosses than to quit their jobs.

As individuals and groups break out of the norm by taking risks, reassure them they are doing the right thing. Although they may not always find immediate success, you can still call it a win. Reinforce their efforts so that they have the where-withal to look forward versus the fear of looking back.

What exactly is a small win? Here are some examples:

- A grumpy teacher smiled.
- A struggling student passed a test.
- A teacher thanked a bus driver.
- A student picked up a small piece of trash.
- Someone shared a funny story at a faculty meeting.
- Mr. Smith combed his hair.

A small win is something that may seem minor when looking at the big picture, but is actually a big deal to someone. It is not an accident or a coincidence. It is a purposeful effort of someone to take that first step toward a new role in life. Your job is to protect that movement.

Showing interest

You cannot just move people forward by using logic. Emotion is an essential part of the process also. Showing individuals that you value them for who they are, not just what they do, is a needed part of moving faculty and staff, and eventually the entire organization forward. This is something a few people try to fake. When that happens, caring becomes difficult to sustain, only to make things worse.

The personal touch goes a long way. Rather than just inquiring about the curriculum change you are hoping for, asking a staff member how his children are doing or how his son is getting along in college can really make that personal link. By sincerely caring and showing that you care, you give others the strength to go beyond their normal parameters. You also provide them with an attachment to you that makes them want to return the support you regularly offer.

If the culture of your school never believed that caring (for each other or for students) was worth the emotional investment, any first attempt at caring may be met with awkward reactions. Cynical people will believe you have an ulterior motive. Some may resist your effort at caring so as not to feel obliged to return it. Some may feel they are now one of your favorite teachers and can get away with anything. But don't let this stop you. Just move slowly.

Building new stories

Underestimating the power of storytelling is a tremendous mistake that leaders often make. Instead of just letting the teacher's lounge anthology carry forth the legends of the school, make sure that positive people are engaged in the process. Cultures are built on and around stories. Stories can influence teacher behaviors more than any policy.

For example, tell a story about something a parent said regarding a teacher who showed a personal touch. Describe how a positive phone call affected a parent's relationship with the school. Let teachers know how students describe them or their class with great enthusiasm. And guess what: the story doesn't need to be true. We are not asking you to lie; we are asking you to shed light on a vision. This approach can let everyone know that doing the right thing, going the extra mile, showing special concern is really what makes a difference. It is what makes this school different. *Be a story.* Tell it through your actions so that everyone knows what is valued. The emotional magnitude of this effort can affect others in an incredibly rich and meaningful way.

When to Quit

Sometimes people need to know that you will stop ineffective practices from happening, occasionally even before they start. As a school leader your job is to protect your faculty as much as it is to serve students. You have the keys to the culture, and the culture is the security blanket that people run to in times of insecurity and confusion. The challenge is knowing when to stop doing something that is not working. You may be the only one who can see the failure, even when the culture is telling everyone it will work.

Here is an analogy to consider. Whenever you load a new program onto your computer, you always have the option to "quit" as it loads. The quit button will be available to the task manager throughout the process. And then, once loaded, the program will ask you to restart your computer—a final commitment that announces to the whole system that something new has been allowed to influence activity. We wonder, what might cause someone to push the quit button as a new program is loading? And why might installers refuse to reboot the whole system to allow the new program to become functional?

We hope this computer analogy has not chased you away from reading more.

Let's connect the computer images to school leadership. First, what might cause a school leader to "quit" a new program even though the program never had a chance to be implemented? Why does the culture not see a failure when something is not working? In the computer world, we might push the quit button in the event that the new program does one of the following:

- Takes too long to load

- Detects a virus

- Triggers too many pop-ups as it loads

- Requires too much personal information

- Indicates incompatibility with the current system

- Takes too much space on the hard drive

Most of these issues become apparent *as the loading occurs*, not so much before the decision to try it out. Many nefarious programs will not disclose their full intentions until the installer has made some level of commitment; then such programs may camouflage the quit button or make promises that seem too good to be true. Is it possible for us to look at this list through the lens of school leadership? Let's give it a try.

- **Takes too long to load.** Here we have the typical problem with many programs that promise improvements: they require a long time for the implementation to reach a point of fidelity. As the new program (e.g., a change in board policy, a new curriculum, a scheduling experiment) is "loaded" into the system, people may become restless and impatient as they wait for signs of improvement.

Sometimes an implementation dip or a novelty spike can occur, which can skew the required wait time. Either way, a regression to the mean can be expected. In terms of school culture, this is a statistician's way of telling us the culture will get its way as things return to normal over time. We will push the quit button when the initiative takes too long to become useful.

- **Detects a virus.** Sometimes our intuition kicks in (it is really the culture whispering in our ear) and tells us that this is a bad idea and must be stopped before it can do any damage. That feeling we get in the pit of our stomachs before any new event that requires a large investment can cause false negatives to influence our attitudes toward anything (everything) new. Change is a virus to culture. The culture will cause discomfort (give you a fever) to protect the system from the virus.

- **Triggers too many pop-ups as it loads.** A pop-up is a distracting new window that suddenly pops up on the screen as a new program loads. These are commercials designed to distract the installer from quitting the installation, or to tempt the installer to upgrade to (spend more money on) a better program, or perhaps to make links to similar products easier to access. For school leaders, pop-ups may be the noise caused by the demands of the job vying for attention, whether it be individuals posturing to appear "on board" with the new program or past practices attempting to discredit a new practice. Issues pop up all the time. The challenge is to not let them distract us from the new investment.

- **Requires too much personal information.** When we are asked to disclose personal information, there comes a point when we feel too much information is being shared. This causes vulnerability. Now trust becomes an issue. To be "all in" with a new program can quickly require a real-location of personal time and a shift in personal patterns of life that were not evident in the beginning discussions. Once we fully commit to something, we tend to hang onto it, even if it fails (Lindstrom, 2008). Unfortunately, we sometimes reach a point when our pride will not let us stop something we have heavily invested in.

- **Indicates incompatibility with the current system.** Simply put, the culture doesn't like it. If the new stuff does not resemble the old stuff, then it will have a difficult time being accepted or implemented at full capacity. Thus it is sabotaged before it ever starts. Leaders may sense this dynamic before the commitment becomes too much. In this scenario, the culture wins and becomes stronger for when the next new thing arrives.

- **Takes too much space on the hard drive.** The school schedule is sacred. People become used to doing their work within particular time frames. We become efficient at getting what needs to be done during normal working hours. When it appears that something new may be asking some workers to show up early or stay late, voices from many agencies will cry foul. Leaders can avoid these voices by quitting on the installation.

We can only do so much. To operate beyond 100 percent is an oxymoron when it comes to the real job of educators—caring. The new stuff can become too big as it infiltrates workloads. When we find organizations asking their members to increase their productivity, the typical incentive will be extrinsic in nature, as if workers were holding back, waiting for more money. Once the "installation" is complete, the leader must now reboot the whole system to allow everyone to recognize it is here and ready to go. On a computer, this may involve simply pressing the enter key. In leadership, this may be something a bit more dramatic. Unfortunately, in the real world we cannot stop everything to allow something new to get a grip. In the real world it is more like being on the on-ramp of a highway than installing a new program on a computer. Once we are on the highway, it may be a while before we can exit (uninstall). Quitting publicly may cost something in social capital and reputation.

We are not asking leaders never to push the quit button. Sometimes we can be fooled into buying something that is not useful. Sometimes weak programs can be disguised as effective programs through the use of strategic testimonials or vague statistics. Once such flaws are discovered, prudent school leaders will stop bad programs from downloading into their systems. We just want school leaders to know that sometimes the decision to quit on something new—perhaps before it ever had a chance to make a difference—can come from voices in the system that should not have a vote. Cultures are designed to detect viruses, which typically come labeled as change—any change. If the culture has a loud voice, the quit button is almost the size of the whole screen.

When is it time to quit? Simply put, when good people don't like something or when weak people support it.

Culture Protects People, People Protect Culture

As we work to improve people by improving culture and as we work to improve culture by improving people, we must also be aware of an important dynamic: not only does the culture not want to change, many people feel the same way. In your school, someone may toss out an idea that clearly would have a positive effect on students. You would think that people would naturally and enthusiastically jump on board. But what happens is many (if not most) use their self-filter, and their first thought is, "How does that affect me?" If the proposal may result in more work, hassle, or stress, they may immediately work to keep the change from occurring.

Now, the culture may not allow them to exclaim, "I am inherently lazy, and I will not get a stipend, so count me out!" but instead require them to say, "We have so many initiatives going on simultaneously, let's wait and see how some of these get implemented, and then in a few years we can revisit that concept."

When school districts attempt to pass referendums, seldom do opponents openly exclaim, "We do not really care about children or the community; thus I will vote against the proposal to build a new school and hire additional teachers." Community norms and culture seldom allow for such a response. Instead opponents may say something like this: "If we were building two small schools rather than one large one, or if we were not including a swimming pool, then I would be in favor."

Hiding behind cultural norms protects people from being more vulnerable and targeted. These same things happen at the school level. Being aware of this dynamic increases a leader's ability to remove some of the excuses and offer support as things change. This is one reason why when a new idea is introduced we do not share the negatives or downsides of that concept. People who do not want to enter new territory quickly use those excuses as a shield. We must be aware of the negatives of a new concept—or at least make resisters work to come up with them on their own!

Why Ineffective People
Seldom Ask for Assistance

We often wonder why people who are ineffective do not work harder to find guidance. Perhaps they do not know they are ineffective. This may be true in some circumstances, but most ineffective teachers do not just close the door to their classrooms; they paper over the window so no one can look in!

An even more likely reason is that being ineffective means others do the work for them. We know they will botch a task if we ask them to do it, so we do not ask them to do it. Their ineffectiveness becomes a self-fulfilling prophecy. Typically in most settings the culture allows this to happen. We must stop these practices by pairing the importance of the task with the skill level of the people. Rather than asking some people to do nothing and others to do almost everything, we must rebalance things by making sure everyone has at least a share of the work. It is not reasonable to have all things divided equally, but we need to make sure that everyone has a part that is proportional to their talent. By making these decisions on a regular and appropriate level, we enable the culture to be the manager and allow the leader to provide the guidance that every organization truly needs.

/ / / / / / /

In the next chapter we shift away from leadership and management to a clearer focus on people—specifically, on improving job satisfaction and morale. These topics are nothing new to the challenging world of school leadership. What is new is learning where satisfaction and morale actually reside and the best approaches to improving both. Leaders too often have to repair the damage that they or other leaders have done themselves. Sometimes such damage is called change. Culture owns satisfaction and morale, so don't try to bring donuts to the faculty lounge and expect everything to get better. It is essential that there be a continual and intentional effort to move people, the school, and the culture down a better path. Such an effort allows people to celebrate every day and takes away inherent excuses to be unhappy on a certain day of the week or time of the year.

CHAPTER 14

Cultivating
Culture to
Improve Job
Satisfaction
and Morale

Every school has a few people who are the most talented and a few who are the most influential. The world works best when these two groups overlap as much as possible.

ere we'll look at two concepts that have been heavily researched: job satisfaction and morale. We believe it is difficult to have one of these be good and the other not be good. They are linked conceptually and intuitively. But we won't spend much time actually talking about the theories behind these concepts as much as we will look at the practical application and influence that can be felt when these concepts are strong or weak. Our goal is not to improve your school morale, but rather to empower you to improve it using the force that matters most, school culture.

You will find an activity that can be used alone, with small groups, or with the whole faculty. We hope the people in your school will become more aware of the school's culture and thus better at asking the right questions. We believe the best questions will have the solution hidden in them. Remember, culture is never a problem to be solved; it is the means we use to solve problems.

When the Culture Is Strongest

When do we leave culture alone? When it is doing its thing—providing security to its members. We have discussed times when the culture is vulnerable and when it is easiest to modify aspects of the culture. We believe there are also times when the culture is strongest, and any attempt to make modifications during these times would put the person trying to make the changes in a difficult position.

There are times during the school year when the culture is flexing its muscle, making everyone who is part of the group feel good about being a member. There are times when a member receives a deserved award and thanks the group. There are times when a teacher may be at the receiving end of a parent's verbal assault and the faculty stand behind her. There may be times when the whole group is standing in unison ready to fight. Think about the times when your culture is strongest:

- Graduation
- Sports banquets
- School recognition events
- When state test results are returned
- When a teacher is threatened

Now, as you know, culture being strong is not inherently good or bad. It depends on what type of a culture it is. As we've said many times, culture is the organization's personality. We all know individuals who have a strong personality. Sometimes it is a *good* strong, other times, not so much. A strong personality can be situationally beneficial or harmful. The same thing applies to a culture. The strength is not a judgment of quality as much as it is a descriptor of magnitude.

But there are times when the culture pulls together in a positive fashion and delivers benefits in the form of changing the outliers who may not be making positive choices. As a culture develops or evolves by making decisions based on what is best for students, it naturally tugs at those who are not doing this. Think about an event as simplistic as a student assembly. Are there differences between what the best teachers do at assemblies and what the less productive teachers do at assemblies? Typically, what do the most engaged teachers do at assemblies? They sit by their students. But rather than sit by their students randomly, they *coincidentally* sit by those students who might be most likely to be talkative or disruptive. Now picture what the least engaged teachers do at assemblies. They might sit in the back, stand against the wall, sit with other teachers, or not even attend the assembly.

If new teachers join the faculty and have been given no guidance, they will either walk into the first assembly and observe what their colleagues are doing or be told by peers what the unwritten rules are about teacher behavior at assemblies. If it seems like the majority or maybe even a minority of teachers from their grade level or department are choosing a certain approach, they are likely to do the same. This is how culture works. It spreads the unwritten rules and expectations to new initiates. It doesn't matter what the new teachers read in the teacher handbook at that point. Even if the new teachers do the right thing by sitting near their challenging students the first time, some of their peers may whisper in their ear, "That's not what we do here. We all just sit together in the back." Thus the culture has influenced, in a negative manner, young teachers' behavior, possibly forever or at least until they realize they have a choice.

But if the principal, before the first assembly, helps new faculty understand the importance of anticipating misbehavior and being preventative by using proximity to improve students' assembly behavior, the practice of many staff members may be different. This could affect the new teachers when they go to their first assembly. Now they look at colleagues who are sitting by students rather than hunkering down in the back of the auditorium and this becomes their norm, even if that is not what took place at the school where they did their student teaching.

Because culture resides in our minds, even a conversation between the administrator and the new teachers could help them become a catalyst in helping shape a new routine. Leaders need to help lead people while guiding the culture in a positive direction, and then the power of culture will help to positively mold new faculty. First steps can be to develop small groups of teachers who are willing to move in a positive direction, even if the overall culture lags. If the principal meets with the new staff members and explains assembly expectations, they may feel protected enough within their developing subculture to make correct decisions.

When teachers make decisions that improve student behavior, they give a powerful boost to job satisfaction and morale. A leader who makes clear what is expected does a great deed for new teachers who want to do what is right. If the leader offers no guidance, then the culture will definitely light the path for them. Sometimes that light points toward the right way and sometimes toward the wrong way, but without the leader providing directionality, the culture is always happy to lead people into the past.

The Problem with Culture Is That It Is Not a Problem

Often morale is expressed as a response to how problems are addressed. All organizations face problems, and if those problems are handled well, people don't mind facing the next one. If they are not handled well, people will do whatever they can to avoid the next problem.

As we have said repeatedly, organizational culture is not a problem that needs to be solved; it is the way people solve problems. If the culture stinks, we are basically stating that the culture does not know how to solve problems. Sometimes cultures *need* problems to maintain the status quo, just so they can play that card when needed. Thus some school cultures can keep problems from being solved. The easiest way to do that is either to declare a problem not a problem (declare it to be a part of "who we are") or to rely on recollections of past failures to thwart any future attempts to fix it.

The problem may be in the way your school defines "problem." Is a problem something that keeps you from reaching your goals or simply something that makes you uncomfortable?

Here is a problem for which many school cultures claim to have an answer. Schools often struggle with or revisit policies involving student behavior. One approach is to revise the student discipline code constantly. Yes, the government creates new standards with which we must comply, but this conversation transcends that. The challenge is making sure we ask ourselves what our goal is. Is the goal to develop a new student discipline code (compliance), or is our goal to improve student behavior?

These are very different goals that may or may not even be related. If our goal is to improve student behavior, then, unfortunately, it requires us to improve adult behavior. Any time we ask adults to change their behavior, the culture becomes resistant. If we are trying to alter adult behavior in a school, we are, at a minimum, required to tweak the culture. (How often have you wondered if some teachers are the cause of student misbehavior? Perhaps we should stop trying to fix the kids if they are just responding to a negative environment we have thrown them into.)

Thus, cultures may respond to the need for a new student behavior plan by creating new plans—problem solved. If the culture wants to improve student behavior, then that school will look at all factors contributing to the problem, which may include teacher behaviors.

Cultures are usually not good at finding problems. Cultures exist to protect what is currently happening. Finding problems provides ammunition to criticize the current status, which may invoke conversations about change. The only problem a culture may acknowledge is when people state there is a problem. "If they aren't happy, then they can leave," say most cultures.

Which of the following would your school categorize as something that defines "who we are" and not as something that could be changed?

- Students from low socioeconomic status community

- Apathetic parents

- Low test scores

- Focus on athletics, not academics

- Unbalanced teacher evaluation process

- Limited budget

Are there schools facing the same issues yet having success? What are the differences between those schools and yours? How did those schools overcome or move past these limitations while your school sees them as impenetrable blockades? As an example, let's take a quick look at poverty.

Poverty presents many challenges to students and their families. Obviously this then has an effect on schools. Many schools find themselves facing higher and higher numbers of students from low-income households who also perform at low levels. (We wonder how many teachers would be upset if their school suddenly enrolled higher numbers of students who are from high-income households and perform at high levels?) Many schools share concerns about meeting the needs of their changing student populations. What has worked previously, in our minds, no longer seems to be as effective. Well, there is a chance whatever it was we were doing never worked with high-need students, but what is different is that we now have more high-need students. Additionally, schools may be less inclined to allow students to fall through the cracks of support than before, given a larger and possibly more visible population.

Some cultures may find strength by gathering around the belief that poverty is an external problem or a societal problem. Doing so may allow teachers to justify that their practices are still working with the "good" kids from "high-quality" homes, and until the poverty levels improve there is nothing that can be done with limited resources, increasing demands, lower pay, increased accountability, and so on. The culture in the school can actually provide a shield for the staff members who are most resistant to change.

However, many schools have moved beyond "excusedom" and realize there are ways to reach these students. They notice that some schools with similar demographics are having much more success than they are; or even closer to home, that some teachers within their own setting are having "luck" with students that others seem to struggle with. This isolated success may allow the culture to become weaker or more fragmented. It can also lend itself to the beginnings of a more collaborative environment. As more teachers accept that they have a higher level of responsibility for student progress, they may be more willing to seek out others in the school who seem to have made progress. The culture can eventually develop to the point that complaining about students' backgrounds starts to ring hollow in the school.

Providing comparisons can also be beneficial. In some schools people compare themselves only to people who are more fortunate than they are. They compare their salaries only with those in districts with higher pay scales. They get upset when a neighboring district has a snow day and they do not, and then get upset when they have to make up a snow day when another district did not lose a day. These responses are often dictated by culture and become normal, even if they seem sad or almost comical to an outsider. How many times have we shared the behavior of a colleague with a spouse or a friend who is not in education and had the listener respond by saying that person would be fired in most companies or organizations? Listeners who work outside of the school world may actually have a more accurate view of what a culture is and what it should be.

The comparisons become important because they can shed light on how we match up with others. It's amazing how many schools describe themselves as "high poverty." When we delve deeper into the numbers, some "suffer" with a 19 percent free-and-reduced-lunch rate. Once they learn that the national rate in 2015 was 51 percent (Rich, 2015), such information can be helpful in altering the dialogue or conversation in a school. Regardless of what their percentage is, helping people find others who are not as fortunate as they are, yet still successful, can begin to alter their understanding and awareness of their own circumstances. We often struggle against the concept of "that's the way we have always done it." By identifying schools and people who share our challenges but have successfully overcome them, we can discover paths through and around the historical dynamic that we may be a part of.

You may be thinking, what if a school's poverty rate is 90-plus percent? Then the challenge can be approached by focusing on what a difference teachers can make every day, how essential it is that they be effective because they may be many students' best hope. The point isn't that all schools are the same—far from it. The goal is to help move the culture and teacher perspective in a way that can help influence others within the culture to make needed changes and improvements for students.

Always remember that culture is in our minds. Altering a mindset, even if it is a few people at a time, can go a long way toward significantly moving an organization in the right direction. But if we do not understand the role of school culture when the topic is (*fill in the topic*), it can be a barrier to making needed progress.

One of the challenges with culture is to ensure that culture is not used as an excuse, particularly by leaders. Too often leaders who are less effective hide behind things like "There is nothing I can do because of the union" or "My hands are tied due to the school board." These statements may or may not be true to some degree, but by thinking this way—or, more harmful, declaring this to others—it reinforces the culture as something that cannot be altered and influenced, and that can become a frightening barrier to doing what is needed in an organization.

Satisfaction is relative to the expectations we have. If the culture has low expectations, then being satisfied comes easily. Morale is more about loyalty to a culture than the way we really feel. If what we do is accepted and valued by our peers, then we feel pretty good and will keep doing it. We won't want to leave. Weighing and recognizing the morale of everyone in a school is important. Being aware of the morale of the critical players is essential. Every school has a few people who are the most talented and a few who are the most influential. The world works best when these two groups overlap as much as possible.

Prioritizing Tasks

We suggest that you try the following activity with your staff. We have used it with success in our principal-prepartion courses and internships.

Provide staff members with a list of 10 tasks (problems) that have come up in a very short period of time. Their job is to prioritize these tasks, to determine which one they will address first, second, third, and so on. Some tasks may seem to be the obvious number-one priority and some may seem silly and easily become the last. But maybe not.

We have found it interesting to compare what leaders prioritize with what the teachers believe to be most important. The information gained from the activity is not so much about who is correct, but rather the degree of congruence among all the adults in the building. In addition, the results become a statement about the values of the school culture. Remember, satisfaction happens when problems are solved the way we expect them to be solved.

Here is a sample of an activity sheet you might use:

> Prioritize the following 10 tasks that have suddenly come to your attention. A #1 means you will address that one first, a #10 means that is the least important task—it can wait.

___ When you walk past a kindergarten classroom, you see the substitute teacher using her cell phone.

___ The custodian wants you to approve the seating in the gym for the afternoon assembly.

___ An adult you do not recognize is coming into the front door of the building.

___ You smell fresh-baked cinnamon rolls.

___ There is laughter coming from the boys' restroom.

___ The superintendent phones and asks if he can observe a teacher with you.

___ The librarian tells you a certain teacher is late with her class coming to use the library—again.

___ A student with special needs is standing in the hallway alone.

___ You glance in a mirror and your hair is a mess.

___ A teacher invites you into her class to watch a student presentation.

For future activities, develop your own list of 10 tasks that may be more relevant to the issues you have faced recently. Be sure to include a few silly, but true, options.

/ / / / / / /

In the next chapter we go beyond job satisfaction and morale to address a broader concept: making teaching "cool" again. What role does culture play in shifting society's perceptions of the teaching profession?

CHAPTER 15

Developing a
Culture Where
Teaching Is
Cool Again

All we can do is tell positive stories, and when people hear educational critics blasting teachers, we can ask them how they got so smart.

Back in the 1970s it was not cool to be in the military. During the Vietnam War era, many would be embarrassed to show up in uniform with a short haircut. But that has all changed in the 21st century. Now those who wear a uniform in public are praised, thanked, hugged—maybe someone even buys their dinner. It is now cool to be in the military.

Back in the 1970s it was cool to be a teacher. People respected what you did and assumed you had high moral standards and could be trusted. By the 21st century, that changed. Many teachers are not quick to share their choice of profession at social gatherings. Teachers have become the convenient reason for anything that seems to be a societal problem. The trust has eroded due to many factors. Simply put, teaching is not cool anymore.

Research has found that teachers in some places will not encourage their children to become teachers (England, 2015). The culture of education is changing to one that requires educators to look over our shoulders. We are playing too much defense against a team (policymakers) that is controlling the scoreboard.

Certainly if we look into the wrong places we can find many reasons to become disenchanted with the profession of teaching. Yet some schools are able to maintain teaching as a profession, rather than just a job. And we find people becoming teachers—good people, who want to make a difference. What can we do to keep them proud? What is happening to the others, and what can we do for them?

We have to remind faculty and staff continually that what we do makes a difference each day. What educators do is not easy, but the good teachers didn't choose education because it was easy. They chose education because it is significant, essential, and life changing. Making sure that as school leaders we continue to share how lucky we are, how thankful we are, and how fortunate we are to be educators is a song we need to play and replay. We cannot control the negative messages people hear from outside our schools. All we can do is tell positive stories, and when people hear educational critics blasting teachers, we can ask them how they got so smart.

Many outside agencies—state departments of education, elected officials—have made educators feel we are under attack, as have developments related to such things as test scores and new evaluation processes. The list is quite lengthy. We must always keep in mind that no matter what else happens when a teacher and students are alone in the classroom, there can be something special happening every day. That is what really matters. That is what students will remember. That is what makes a difference.

Remembering that culture is in our minds, we can conclude that it is impossible to change a culture using only logic. It is essential that emotion be a part of the effort. We can share stories, celebrate accomplishments, work to remember why we chose education. We can be that light that everyone is drawn to rather than someone whom people avoid. When times are such that few people are choosing to work in education, there will be a greater opportunity to be that oasis that attracts the best talent to your school. Only the best will want to be teachers despite the lack of societal support. The need for teachers will increase as fewer choose it as a profession. This could be a quality control measure in disguise.

Establishing Your School's Brand

As we try to help educators understand the environments we have created for students, we can find unique ways to describe those environments. In this activity we ask you and your staff to describe your school using the following prompts:

- A texture, or degree of grit

- Five themes or terms

- Quotes from the past that still echo in the halls

- The type of guard at the front door (e.g., sentry, monster, lawyer)

- A kind of food (e.g., fast food, eatery, mid-level chain, home cooking)

- A contemporary fable, using local jargon

- A sport (e.g., boxing, golf, baseball)

- A movie, assigning a few key roles

- A kind of TV show (e.g., drama, sitcom, game show)

You can use your responses to develop an overall image of the type of setting you are asking your students to succeed in. We anticipate that some humor will emerge from this discussion, as well as some new insights that may serve to help you and your staff rethink some of the things that happen at your school: why do they happen, who is letting them happen, should we change them, and who owns the change?

Rekindling Pride

Educators make a difference and have so much to be proud of. Sometimes it is easy to forget that. We have to ensure that a positive, collaborative school culture is established and continually replenished that can make everyone in our schools feel special. Our teachers need such affirmation. Our students deserve it.

///////

Help teachers feel that first-year excitement again. Let your culture do most of the work when it comes to improving people. Culture never sleeps, and it wants you to be proud of what you do. And let your best people do most of the work to improve the culture. It's what they do.

CHAPTER 16

Concluding
Thoughts

Align the culture with the
mission and vision.

As we close this book, we have a few additional thoughts to share with you. These ideas are still floating around in our heads and we ask that you give them a chance to stir your thinking.

Culture, Mission, or Vision: Which One Is Running Your School?

Many school leaders will espouse their mission and vision as the driving forces in their schools. We argue it is more about the culture of the school, and this culture will interpret the mission and vision despite the efforts of any think tank or committee. If the culture is aligned with the mission and vision, then your school is a great place and you should anticipate great things to come. If there is misalignment, the culture will win. We are not asking you to align the mission and vision with the culture. We need you to consider just the opposite: align the culture with the mission and vision.

Let's try to rephrase what we just stated. We need you to lead the effort among you and your colleagues to align (1) what you do with (2) why you are here and (3) who you want to be.

We're not sure if that helped, but basically, if you do not know what you "do around here," why you keep coming to school, and what you want the school to look like in five years, then the culture will make that decision for you. It will make the next five years look like the last five years.

Whatever people "do around here" is usually what is easiest to do. There is a path of least resistance that allows each of us to continue doing what we have always done. Each time we do it, we validate it. The mission tells us why we do it, and the vision should tell us whether or not what we are doing is good enough. The culture is trying to make sure neither the mission nor the vision interrupts what we are already doing.

Understanding Cultural Distance to Reduce Culture Shock

Here we borrow from the world of ethnography and look at the concept of cultural distance. In essence, cultural distance increases when the values and beliefs of one group contrast with those of another group. The less two groups have in common, the greater the cultural distance. What this means for the purposes of this book is realizing that some schools are really different from other schools when we compare their cultures. Sometimes two schools that are 5 miles apart have a larger cultural distance than two schools that are 100 miles apart.

Given this cultural distance that may occur between two schools, is it possible that some people may not adapt quickly to the next place they work, experiencing culture shock? More relevant, will some teachers new to your school be easier to influence (assimilate) than others? These new teachers can be first-year teachers or veteran teachers from other schools. Cultures try to assimilate everybody. Yet some people will come to a new school and think, "Wow, these people are weird." The sense of "weirdness" usually goes away in a few weeks—at least for most people.

The ones who continue to think it is a weird place may be the resources you need for change. A good way to kill learning is to reward those who fit in with the status quo—provided the status quo is not the best possible situation. Perhaps there is an optimal cultural distance that needs to be considered when hiring the next person.

When to Listen to Culture, When to Ignore Culture

What has happened in the past will give us some idea as to what needs to happen in the future. Our successes and failures will help us to get better. The voice of culture is the voice of the past. Imagine an elderly gentleman sitting next to a fireplace, slowly rocking in a chair with a blanket over his lap, staring at the flames. In this dimly lit room we can imagine him reminiscing about the special events of his life. If we approach this person with a question, the typical response may begin with, "Well, in my day. . . ." This is the role many school cultures play. These cultures provide craft wisdom from a time long past. And although they may include some useful thoughts, chances are the past has been altered a bit each time the same story is told.

We hope you do not feel like we just called your grandfather a liar. We have much to respect about people who have experienced many of life's blessings and tragedies and who come out better people. We believe most school cultures make good decisions most of the time. If they did not, the schools would be closed. Our argument here is that sometimes the culture does not provide for the best decision, not because it does not care about the future, but because it does not have the capacity to deal with uncertainty. If there is doubt about what to do next, the culture will bring up something (relevant or not) that worked in the past as a solution. Sometimes it feels better to do what we have always done rather than to solve the actual problem—like bringing a hammer to help someone replace a car windshield.

The quicker the future comes at us, the less relevant the past becomes. What happens when we face problems that did not exist five years ago? It is popular to announce to the world that we are educating people for jobs that do not yet exist, yet many of those people are heading back to the classrooms and providing instruction that resembles the 1950s.

If a problem persists, it may be because the culture is unable to find a tool it does not already have. This is when we look to our most effective people—new teachers and veterans—and trust them with our options, without disrespecting those who built the past.

///////

The relationship between people and culture is incredibly complex and inarguably important. Which one is the cause of changes and which one is affected varies from situation to situation. However, there is no disputing that each has a direct and indirect connection with the other. School leaders must be attuned and sensitive to this dynamic. We must always remember that they can pull each other up in a positive direction or push each other down. By working on one, we affect the other. By ignoring one, we harm the other. Being intentional in what we do will make a tremendous difference in our people and our schools. It is critical that we take on the challenge. It is one worthy of our best effort. Culture always wins. And when a positive culture wins, so do our students.

REFERENCES

Brown, B. (2015). *Daring greatly: How the courage to be vulnerable transforms the way we live, love, parent, and lead.* Knoxville, TN: Avery.

Collins, J. (2001). *Good to great: Why some companies make the leap . . . and others don't.* New York: HarperCollins.

Cruz, L. (2015). *Transforming school culture: Exploring effective principal school leadership.* Keynote address presented at the Annual Fall Conference of the Indiana Association of School Principals.

Deal, T., & Kennedy, A. (1982). *Corporate cultures: The rites and rituals of corporate life.* New York: Addison-Wesley.

Dewey, J. (1938/1993). *Experience and education, 60th anniversary ed.* Kappa Delta Pi: Indianapolis, IN.

England, E. S. (2015). *The relationship among reasons teachers entered the profession, job satisfaction, and encouraging future teachers.* Unpublished dissertation, Indiana State University, Terre Haute.

Fullan, M. (2014). *The principal: Three keys to maximizing impact.* San Francisco: Jossey-Bass.

Fullan, M., & Quinn, J. (2016). *Coherence: The right drivers in action for schools, districts, and systems.* Thousand Oaks, CA: Corwin.

Glasser, W. (1998). *Choice theory: A new psychology of personal freedom.* New York: Harper Collins.

Gruenert, S., & McDaniel, T. (2009). The making of a weak teacher. *The School Administrator, 66*(10), 30.

Gruenert, S., & Whitaker, T. (2015). *School culture rewired: How to define, assess, and transform it.* Alexandria, VA: ASCD.

Hargreaves, A. (2015, Autumn). Push, pull and nudge: The future of teaching and educational change. *LEARNing Landscapes, 9*(1), 119.

Heath, C., & Heath, D. (2007). *Made to stick: Why some ideas survive and others die.* New York: Random House.

Lewin, K. (1936). *Principles of topological psychology.* New York: McGraw-Hill.

Lindstrom, M. (2008). *Buyology: Truth and lies about why we buy.* Crown Business: New York.

Maslow, A. H. (1943). A theory of human motivation. *Psychological Review. 50* (4): 370–396. Accessed http://psychclassics.yorku.ca/Maslow/motivation.htm.

Rich, M. (2015, Jan. 16). Percentage of poor students rise. *New York Times*. Accessed. http://www.nytimes.com/2015/01/17/us/school-poverty-study-southern-education-foundation.html?_r=0.

Treasurer, B. (2014). *Leaders open doors* (2nd ed.). Danvers, MA: American Society for Training & Development (ASTD).

Turner, E. A. (2013). *What effective principals do to improve instruction and increase student achievement.* Unpublished dissertation, Indiana State University, Terre Haute.

Whitaker, T., Whitaker, B., & Lumpa, D. (2013). *Motivating and inspiring teachers: The educational leader's guide for building staff morale* (2nd ed.). New York: Routledge.

INDEX

The letter *f* following a page number denotes a figure.

ABOUT THE AUTHORS

Steve Gruenert is a professor at Indiana State University. He has studied organizational culture and climate for more than 20 years and continues to learn and collaborate with other researchers as these concepts evolve. Steve is the coauthor of *School Culture Rewired: How to Define, Assess, and Transform It* and *Minds Unleashed: How Principals Can Lead the Right-Brained Way*. He has three daughters, Jennifer, Mackenzi, and Madison. His wife Emily also works at Indiana State University as a student advisor.

Todd Whitaker has been fortunate to be able to blend his passion with his profession. He is a leading presenter in the field of education. Todd is a professor of educational leadership at the University of Missouri and professor emeritus at Indiana State University. He has worked as a teacher and a principal and is the author or coauthor of more than 40 books, including *School Culture Rewired, What Great Teachers Do Differently, Your First Year,* and *Shifting the Monkey*. Todd and his wife Beth have three children: Katherine, Madeline, and Harrison.

Related ASCD Resources: School Culture

At the time of publication, the following ASCD resources were available (ASCD stock numbers in parentheses). For up-to-date information about ASCD resources, go to www.ascd.org. Search the complete archives of *Educational Leadership* at www.ascd.org/el.

ASCD EDge® Group
Exchange ideas and connect with other educators interested in school culture including *Let's Talk School Culture and Climate*, and *Change and School Culture* on the social networking site ASCD EDge® at http://ascdedge.ascd .org/

Print Products
How to Create a Culture of Achievement in Your School and Classroom by Douglas Fisher, Nancy Frey and Ian Pumpian (#111014)

Igniting Teacher Leadership: How do I empower my teachers to lead and learn? (ASCD Arias) by William Sterrett (#SF116039)

The Principal 50: Critical Leadership Questions for Inspiring Schoolwide Excellence by Baruti K. Kafele (#115050)

School Climate Change: How do I build a positive environment for learning? (ASCD Arias) by Peter DeWitt and Sean Slade (#SF114084)

School Culture Rewired: How to Define, Assess, and Transform It by Steve Gruenert and Todd Whitaker (#115004)

For more information: send e-mail to member@ascd.org; call 1-800-933-2723 or 703-578-9600, press 2; send a fax to 703-575-5400; or write to Information Services, ASCD, 1703 N. Beauregard St., Alexandria, VA 22311-1714 USA.